C000244743

Barry Cornell was born at a ve
village in northern England w
normal way, eventually graduating to long pants, long
hair and aspirations of rock stardom. His early career in
accountancy came to an abrupt end when he inadvertently dropped Lady Borg Ropner (deceased)'s Fourth
Children's Settlement file down a toilet. He almost had
a normal teaching career until he discovered learning
difficulties and became the Head of a special school. He
and his wife have lived in France since 2002, latterly in
Haute Vienne which they describe to prospective
visitors as the French Midlands, to put them off.
Make Mine a Kilowatt is his first book. He is working on
a sequel.

The illustrator, Mike Evans, spent most of his working
life involved in visual media. Now living in France, he
spends his retirement putting the author's lawn mower
back together after it has been severely abused yet again.
A close friend of Barry and his devoted wife, he is also
committed to convincing them both that divorce is not
the only option.

Make Mine
a Kilowatt!

Bemused, bewildered and bamboozled by life in France

Barry Cornell

Illustrated by Mike Evans

To Shirley and Robert
with best wishes.

MOSAÏQUE PRESS

Mike Evans.

Dec. '4

First published in 2014 by
Mosaïque Press
Registered office:
70 Priory Road
Kenilworth, Warwickshire CV8 1LQ
www.mosaïquepress.co.uk

Printed in the UK.

ISBN 978-1-906852-32-0

For Lyndsay and Dave,
Daisy and Amélie

Contents

Acknowledgements

I WOULD LIKE TO THANK Dan Bessie for his wise observations and advice, I am grateful, too, to Mike Evans for his artistic input. And of course I must recognise the debt I owe to my long-suffering wife, Kath, for tolerating the sometimes unflattering picture I have painted of her, and for putting up with me.

I suppose I should also acknowledge the input of the members of Marval's Total Boules team, who have encouraged me in my writing, even though I constantly beat them, and have contributed to this book in ways they will never know: Archie, Brian, David, the other David, Freddie, Geoff, John, Kevin, Malcolm, Mike, Phil, Richard, Robert, Roger, Ron and Stuart.

Thanks are due to my publisher Chuck Grieve for his faith in me and his support, guidance and friendship, to Penny Drake for introducing us and to Gill Connors for providing the ambience in which a scheme was hatched, the result of which you are holding in your hands.

Countless other friends and strangers have also provided inspiration for my stories over the years. Some people may even imagine they can see elements of themselves in one or two of my caricatures. To them I offer my sincere thanks for just being in my line of sight. To their lawyers I deny everything.

Some of the stories in this book were first published in my regular columns in two of France's English language newspapers, *French News* and *French Life*. As is customary, I would like to acknowledge the support and encouragement of the editors of these publications and to thank them for permission to reprint those stories in this collection, and I would if I knew where to find them, but sadly both newspapers have gone into liquidation. To anyone who thinks they detect a pattern here, with perhaps a whiff of conspiracy, I would just like to point out that the demise of both newspapers in which my column appeared is pure coincidence, to say nothing of ruddy bad luck, and anyone imagining anything sinister is really scraping the bottom of the barrel for a plot.

Nine chips hungry

NOW HERE'S A THING. WHY IS IT that whenever I take my wife to a French restaurant she wants something that isn't on the menu? No matter that the menu runs to fifteen pages and has a choice of forty-six dishes, Kath will always be disappointed that they don't have what she wants. Which inevitably leads to me having to make embarrassing requests such as "Excuse me, Madame, but do you by any chance have mussels with a Provençal sauce and raspberry vinegar? Yes I know this is a pizzeria, but I thought there'd be no harm in asking..."

Worse, she sometimes wants dishes that are all somewhere on the menu, but she doesn't want them in any of the available combinations.

This is where it really gets sticky. My French isn't bad, and I can trot out most of the essential everyday phrases such as "I am so sorry I trod on your child," "Pardon me, but could you repeat that in a language other than *patois* and this time without chewing on your cheroot?" or "I am truly devastated that I do not have the precise amount of coinage necessary to furnish you with the exact cost of this newspaper and have thereby caused you a great inconvenience by suggesting that as a shopkeeper you might actually, just for once in your life, have the facility to give me change from a five euro note."

But it's another thing entirely to have to launch into something like:

"Good evening, Monsieur. My wife, who I should warn you is a dangerous woman to cross, will have the *menu du jour* at fifteen euros, except that she would prefer garlic prawns to start with, and since these are not part of the *menu du jour*, but are instead listed in your *à la carte* at seven euros, I shall be happy for you to augment the bill by an amount which represents the difference between a *menu du jour* starter and seven euros.

"Okay so far? Now, she tells me she is not too keen on crème caramel for dessert and wonders if you could substitute strawberries and cream for it. Again, I will be pleased to meet any reasonable surcharge, although my wife, who is financially astute, does wish me to point out that she does not want any wine, which is included in the price of the *menu du jour,* and therefore you might like to consider offsetting, against the additional cost of the strawberries, an allowance for the wine she won't be drinking.

"Oh yes, and does the main course rabbit come in bits, or whole with its paws on? Because if it's the latter she'd prefer duck.

"To finish she'd like an extremely hot but very weak decaffeinated coffee with non-fat milk, half a sweetener and one of those nice square chocolates, please."

And then to crown it all, having got just what she wants, at the cost of my dignity and equilibrium, she decides that she doesn't much like it anyway and would rather have what I am eating! Not all of it, you understand – for that would be too easy, involving nothing more elaborate than a swift and surreptitious exchange of plates. No, she only wants some parts of it: invariably the parts which I most enjoy.

11

Thus begins an uncivilised bartering session, conducted in aggressive stage whispers with much rolling of eyes and pointing of fingers, followed eventually by The Great Food Exchange. Have you ever tried to sneakily spoon a portion of *boeuf bourguignon* across to the plate opposite and receive in return a half-eaten piece of rabbit paw? All the while maintaining a conversation as if nothing unusual was happening? "Yes, darling, Marion's bum did look big in that new outfit. Whoops, can we try to recover that piece of carrot from the sugar bowl?"

And I always, but always, lose out in the bargain. Many's the time I've sacrificed a juicy bit of sirloin in return for half an onion, or an entire pork chop for a dollop of spinach. I've even been known to surrender a Yorkshire pudding in return for a miserable piece of celery.

But I have my pride, and there is a point beyond which I will not go. And that point arrives when my chips are threatened.

You see, while I like to pretend that I'm a *bon viveur* with a sophisticated palate and a taste for the finest gastronomic creations, I nonetheless have to admit to a fondness for potatoes, or more specifically, chips. I love chips. I can eat enormous quantities of chips without hesitation, repetition or deviation, although I usually settle for just a portion. So when the chips are down, as it were, my chips are mine. They aren't up for grabs. They are non-negotiable. Inviolable. Sacrosanct. A protected species.

You see, if you think about it, a portion of chips, as we understand it in European cultures today, has evolved through the centuries to be of such a quantity that there will be just the right amount for one person. They don't bring you a plate of four chips; nor do they fetch four hundred. Instead, they serve what has gradually become today's

norm in Western European society – say about twenty to twenty-five chips. Perhaps thirty in Belgium. And in just the same Darwinian way, I have evolved to be exactly one person with exactly one person's appetite (though my wife would probably disagree).

So there has emerged a sort of happy correlation between me and the suppliers of chips: I want a portion; they serve a portion. Such beautiful symmetry works not just for me and chips, but for all normal people and all normal suppliers of goods, and means that we can actually buy things in the quantities that we are likely to need. For instance, I have become accustomed to wearing precisely two shoes, and over the years shoe manufacturers have cleverly adapted their production so as to supply them in convenient pairs. *Voila!* In the same way it is surely no coincidence that in B&Q, nails are now sold in packs of ten, which is the very number I require in order to make sure that one of them is knocked in properly. And wine is thoughtfully served in seventy-five centilitre bottles, which correlates exactly with the amount I need to drink with (or without) a meal.

And so it is with chips.

But sadly, my wife doesn't conform to the normal human template. She takes a third of a teaspoon of sugar in her coffee. In France she drives on the right for most of the time. And in the same way she always wants nine chips. Don't ask me why. It must be something in her genes, I think: some evolutionary flaw in her personality, some metaphorical spanner in her works. And of course, you can't order nine chips, can you? You can only order a portion.

So what I reckon she ought to do is order a portion, and then leave most of it. To me, preferably, or failing that, to posterity. But no; that would be wasteful and extravagant, so it's much better for her to order no portions at all and instead raid my portion, invariably filching about nine.

And note I'm not talking about a trade-off here, oh gracious me no. I'm talking about unashamed, unadulterated theft. Now I wouldn't mind too much if she stole just one or two chips – I don't want to be pedantic or mean spirited – but for heavens sake, nine chips is a significant proportion of a chap's meal, is it not? So I lose out, and at the end of the meal I'm still hungry. Not starving, I admit, but still noticeably hungry. And feeling somehow cheated.

I have tried different strategies to overcome this, including wolfing down my chips even as the waiter is putting the plate on the table, swishing at my wife's hand as she reaches over to spear my precious foodstuff, and even, I am ashamed to say, trying to pinion her palm to the table with my fork. But somehow she always prevails.

And I'm always left – precisely – nine chips hungry.

Be my guest

486 Borough Road

Hartlepool

Dear Barry (or is it Barrie?) and Kath,

I don't know if you remember us, because we only met once, at Hilary's party in 2001 (I was the one who was sick in the aquarium, and Stanley entertained everybody with his hilarious Frank Spencer impressions – got it now?)

Anyway, since then we've thought about you a lot, especially since you went to live in France, and we would dearly like to renew our akwaintence and – who knows – maybe even become your best friends.

So we were thinking that when we go to Margate this year for our annuel holiday, since we'll be near Dover, we might just pop over and see you for two or three weeks. It will be nice to see each other again and re-live the lovely time we had at Hilary's 'do'. Stanley has worked hard on his act since then, and he can now nearly do a

brilliant Elvis routine – he's even bought a white suit and sunglasses
and some new sideburns!! Oh you've a treat in store!!

I hope you don't think us forward, but in antisipation of your
agreement we've taken the liberty of booking a ferry crossing on the
8th of July, and we expect to arrive at your house on the 10th in
time for dinner. But you mustn't bother about cooking anything too
special, because we'll already have had a light snack at lunchtime.
Anyway, just to say thank you for your kindness we're going to bring
you a bottle of English wine as a little present, but don't tell Stanley
I told you because he wants it to be a suprise.

Don't know if you remember, but Stanley is a veggitarian and I don't eat bread things and neither of us is keen on salad. But don't worry: we'll just muck in and eat whatever you put in front of us, so long as it's got no meat or fish or bread. Or salad. (And please, none of your fancy French muck!)

If you're wondering what drink to get in, don't bother with wine or anything – Stanley will be quite happy with a few cans of Boddingtons or (if you can get it out there) Newcastle Brown. And rum and cokes for me, as usual – I think they're called koober-leebrers on the Continent.

You're going to adore our family's new 'surprise' addition. Our little Georgie Wayne Rio was born last year, and he is turning into a proper little buster, just like his Dad. He's teathing at the moment, so you won't see him at his best, but even at his worst he's adorible – you'll want to keep him! If you haven't got four bedrooms he can sleep in the same room as our Kylie, whose now turned fifteen and is into all the girlie thing's like pop music and Facebook and body pearcing, and of course she's absolutely MAD on boys – I've told her that you'll know of lots of discos and night clubs to take her to because when she gets bored she can be a right madam! Her probation officer say's she's a little tare-away, but really we reckon she's just high-spirited with perhaps a touch of attention defesit disorder.

We'll be bringing our dogs, of course, but they're no bother. They were just puppies when you saw them at Hilary's, but goodness me how they've grown! The smaller one, Tyson (the rottweiler), is now almost fully toilet traned and a real bundle of fun. Whenever we take his muzzle off he just loves to tare about chasing things.

We're told that you live near a place called Nontron, in the Dordoing, so we're so looking forward to lots of day trips with you to places like Perrygur, Paris and Chammerny. And Niece of course. But Stanley's lost his lisense again and I'm a bit nervous about driving on the wrong side, so you'll have to be the chauffer, I'm afraid. But that means we two girls and the kids can sit in the back and have a good natter about England while Stanley and Barry talk about men's things like football and cage fighting.

Oh, Stanley's just asked me to ask whether you've got a swimming pool, and if so whether it's heated, and is there a jackoozy with it? And he'd also like to know if you've got Sky Sports, because he'd hate to miss any Premiership games if they're televised. I'm just as bad, though – I need my daily fix of telly – Coronation Street, East Enders, the Jeremy Kile show – I just couldn't live without them!

Once we've seen the sights, we can all just chill out and relax. We're told that you've been busy every day for the last four years renevating your house. Well, we know what it's like because Stanley and I have just finished painting our bathroom door, so now what we really want is a complete rest from household chores! Just think: three blissful weeks with no cooking or washing up or shopping or bed-making – I'm so looking forward to it!!

You really must – no, we insist – let us pay something towards our stay, or if you think that's a bit too mersonery (and we're sure you will) then we'd like to show our grattitude at the end by taking you out for one of those special lunches we've read about where you can have five courses for 11 euros. Won't that be exciting!

Well, we'll have to go now because it's nearly time for Holby City and Stanley has to feed the dogs and try to persuade Tyson to drop the cat.

Don't bother to reply; we'll have set off by the time it gets here.

Lots of true love,

Beryl and Stanley (Davison, remember?)

XXX

PS Just wait till we get Stanley started on his jokes! Once he's had a skinfull there's just no stopping him. Did he ever tell you the one about the nun and the rubber chicken?

French chic

ONE OF MY EARLIEST RECOLLECTIONS – I can only have been about four at the time – is of being walked around the streets of Darlington by my grandmother. Nothing unusual in that, you might think. Except that I was dressed in reins. Yes, I said reins. As in Rudolph. I remember the exact design: the straps fit over my shoulders and tied behind my back, from whence a lead (as in Rover) led to my grandmother's hand.

Now it may have been normal in those days, in the late Forties, for young children to wear reins, but I don't think so. None of the photos I've seen of life in those times depicts kids in reins, so I have to assume either that I was an exceptionally unruly child or that, even then, life was conspiring against me to ensure that I would never become a fashion icon.

Things continued in the same vein when I was at primary school. By then the reins had gone, of course, but they had been replaced by a fur-lined mock-leather balaclava. I ask you! It's a wonder I've turned out sane after such a start in life. Yes, it kept my head warm. And my ears. But I didn't want to look like Biggles, I just wanted to be like the other Northern lads – cold but tough. Unfortunately I couldn't pretend to be tough, ever since Gillian Naylor beat me up for pulling her pigtails, but I'm sure I could have made a decent fist of being cold had it not been for my bizarre headwear.

To go to school in those days, lads would wear gabardines – thin navy macs that were supposed to be waterproof – and the trend in Darlington was to wear your gabardine fastened only by the top button. For some reason the top button on these coats was designed to strangle young children by fastening very high and tight around the neck. So by securing only that button and not putting your arms into the sleeves, you could make the coat into a sort of Superman cape, and then of course you could fly and do all sorts of clever tricks and impress those things they called girls.

But how could I ever pass for Superman if I was forced to wear a brown, fur-lined mock-leather balaclava? And worse: I was the last kid in County Durham to graduate into long trousers, so all through those character-forming early years I wore short trousers, grey socks to just below the knee and home-made white elastic garters to keep them up. Garters! It really is amazing that I didn't grow up to be a serial killer or a banker or something.

Secondary school brought no respite. Any hopes I might have entertained of becoming a top Olympic athlete were dashed by the fact that my latest fashion accessory had become – floppy underpants! This was the start of the swinging Sixties, and everybody – even girls as far as I knew – was wearing Y-fronts. Except me. I rapidly decided that I would never willingly undress in front of other lads, and thus relinquished a potential career as a footballer, cricketer or vicar.

So it is only in relatively recent years that I have become the smooth, elegant, fashionable, urbane, devil-may-care man-about-town that I am now. My transformation has been truly remarkable, and stands as a testament to man's ability to overcome tremendous odds. But I have to keep on top of it. There is obviously something in my family's genes that propels us towards wearing outlandish clothing, and who knows, if I let my guard slip for a moment I might find myself wearing a fedora, or a kilt, or a monocle or such-like. So I am always on the lookout for smart, casual, age-appropriate clothing.

By way of example, at the traditional French market in the nearby village of Piégut a couple of months ago I made what I think was a rather splendid purchase. I'd walked briskly past the cheese stall and the inevitable basketwork display, and past the live chickens and the guy selling football club scarves (including Manchester Sitty, Arnesal and – inexplicably – Leighton Orient), and sauntered very slowly past the thong stall (imagine!) And there on the clothes stall I spotted a really nice pullover with a knitted picture of a labrador's head on the front. Or it might have been a cat. Anyway, the point is, this was clearly a one-off. I'd never seen a pullover quite like it. Come to think of it, I'd never seen a labrador's head quite like it either, but it was all done in such exquisite detail, right down to the three dimensional nose (how can anybody be so clever as to knit a sticky-out nose?) and the lovely purple eyes.

This was clearly no mass-produced Marks and Spencer garment, gracious no! It was what they refer to as designer wear, and I knew immediately that I had to have it. I won't tell you the price, because frankly you wouldn't believe it. But I have it, and I'm pleased to say that it seems to be having the desired effect. I wore it at a dinner party last night and everyone was, well, stunned is the word that springs to mind. I caught them on several occasions staring enviously at it. Our

dear friend Pat was almost transfixed. I'm sure she wanted to compliment me on it, but somehow she couldn't find the words.

The old French lady who knits these things is quite prolific and blessed with seemingly endless inspiration. There may never be another labrador pullover, but each week she has a different creation on offer. First there was a sweater incorporating a splendidly knitted picture of a sideways-on penguin (or maybe it was a nun), and then last week another with – I kid you not – a house, and with grey woollen smoke coming out of the chimney and curling up over the shoulder. Eat your heart out, Pierre Cardin.

I must admit I'm tempted by the house pullover. After all, I have my English street cred to maintain, and that's not easy in view of the fact that my dear wife insists on ironing a knife edge crease down the front of my jeans. I ask you, would Paul Newman ever have become a heart-throb with knife-edged jeans? Does anyone else in France, or in the entire world for that matter, have knife-edged jeans? I think not.

Ladies, if you're passing through St Estèphe or Brantôme and happen to see a lithe, bronzed, virile-looking chap sitting nonchalantly at a table, very smartly dressed and looking for all the world like a retired Concorde pilot...

...well, I'll be the guy sitting next to him with the labrador pullover. And those jeans.

Operationment and assemblation instructings made easy

YOU MAY HAVE HEARD THE STORY about the chap who asked the librarian where he could find manuals on how to commit suicide, and received the reply: "We've had to stop lending them, I'm afraid; people just never brought them back."

Well, in my youth I never seemed to have much success with instruction manuals. A lot of these were to do with ways of impressing the opposite sex, and as such promised me great riches. But I remember that even after a most careful study of Victor Sylvester's *Illustrated Guide to Dancing* (I even made notes and practised in front of a mirror) I subsequently failed spectacularly to jive at the Sixth Form Club and had to pretend it was epilepsy.

But I'm grown up now, and therefore instruction manuals no longer hold any terrors for me. For this reason I have somewhat grudgingly condescended to learn how to use the camera I bought my wife for her birthday, just so that I can help her when she encounters problems with it.

She being female, it inevitably follows that she will find great difficulty using such a technically advanced piece of equipment, and I

being male, it naturally follows that I will bail her out when necessary.

And so last Wednesday I sat down to work my way through the camera's instruction booklet. I allowed a good hour and a half, because I wanted to master every intricacy of the machine. It occurred to me to perhaps use the French manual so as to bring a little spice and challenge to the task, but in the end I decided not to add any unnecessary complications to what promised to be a straightforward and simple, if somewhat boring, chore, and so I settled for the English version, which inexplicably seemed to be much longer than the French, the Italian, and even the Dutch.

Well, the thing is this. I didn't just spend an hour and a half. It has actually taken me several days at the last count and, er, I haven't finished. You're probably not going to believe this, I know, but I got sort of bogged down at a fairly early stage. I skipped the EC Declaration of Conformity and the Contents pages, skimmed the Preface and the List of Accessories on page 7, decided to leave the chapter on Nomenclature until after the football season had closed, and raced directly to Page 11: Attaching the Lens Cap and Camera Strap.

Now, should you happen to bump into Kath I'd rather you didn't mention this, but the fact is - astonishingly - I can't damn well do it! Yes, that's right. Me, who was brought up on Meccano sets and, in my later teens, Lego, and who once nearly won a Blue Peter badge for my design for a space ship, defeated by a mere camera! I wrestled, off and on for three and a half days, with the damned lens cap and the sodding strap, and they still remain gloriously and imperiously unattached. I was all right, I think, up to Instruction 4. I had successfully - nonchalantly even - fixed the metal clip things to the sides of the camera, and was just contemplating a celebratory whisky when I came across this little gem:

> Face the black side of the cover towards the camera and attach the strap by threading the strap through the strap clip, starting from the notched side.

This innocuous instruction was accompanied by a childishly simple illustration showing a disembodied hand duly facing the black side of the cover towards the camera and effortlessly attaching the strap by deftly threading the strap through the strap clip, starting – smug bastard – from the notched side. Well, try as I might I just couldn't do it. I bent my fingers and hands into the most hideous contortions trying to do exactly as I was told, but apart from spraining my index finger and dribbling excessively down my shirt, I had no success. And even now the camera, its strap and its lens cap remain determinedly separate. Irreconcilable. Not even speaking to each other.

I think the problem is that I can't find my notch. Oh sure, the picture has a little arrow pointing to what is supposedly a notch, but believe me, there is no corresponding notch on my equipment. Have I, I wonder, been fleeced by the camera chap at Limoges, who is even now boasting to his compatriots of how he has offloaded another notchless Fuji onto an unsuspecting *rosbif?*

So you see my dilemma. Kath is confidently expecting me to coach her through the next 119 pages of the manual, explaining as and when necessary such niceties as Autobracketing for Continuous Shooting, Cancelling DPOF Settings for Specified Frames, and Disabling Signal Processing Functions and Reconstituting the Data Received from the CCD as an Image. Oh boy, I can't wait to get started on that one!

How can I tell her, then, that I can't even fit the bloody strap?

And in the meantime, just to make things worse, I've acquired another set of instructions. I bought a tower – one of those scaffold platforms that allow you to paint the top of your house in absolute comfort and safety – and the instructions for erecting it are all in French. Aaaagh! Oh yes, there are accompanying illustrations. The first one appears to show a six-fingered hand holding half a chopstick and rotating it menacingly through 270 degrees towards a bent ship's propeller. I think I'm doomed.

But surely the worst situation of all is when the instructions aren't in French, or Serbo-Croat, or any known tongue, but are instead in poorly translated English. Yes, I can see you nodding. You know the sort of thing: 'Presently you are mark the trodgel peace with consuming daggers, and finding the erection accomplished with easiness.' I look at such words of wisdom with a sinking heart, knowing with a terrible certainty that I am not going to accomplish the required erection with anything approaching easiness.

In the meantime, would anyone like to buy a camera? With optional strap?

Living in a time warp

WE LIVE NEAR THE LITTLE VILLAGE of St Mathieu, on the edge of the *département* of Haute Vienne, and within the Parc National de Périgord-Limousin. So we can fairly be said to be living in *la France profonde* – deepest France. Think of Swaledale, or perhaps Dartmoor, but with sun.

It is for sure a backward and undeveloped region. There's hardly any public transport, for instance. There aren't any factories, or shopping malls. There isn't much in the way of noise, or bustle, or excitement, or pollution, or progress. There aren't any burglar alarms or CCTV cameras or fast food outlets or football hooligans or motorways. Just farms and lakes and chateaux and old hamlets, and slab-sided cows with velvety hides, and buzzards and boars and bores, and herons and cormorants and... I think you get the picture. Paris it is not. It is neither glamorous nor fashionable, neither sophisticated nor stylish. It's France as it was thirty years ago, or England as it was sixty years ago.

Our British friends who visit sometimes find it a culture shock. Some are overcome by the beauty and tranquillity of the area, the gentleness of the people and the slow pace of life. Others are disappointed by the lack of facilities and activities, miffed that their iPhone won't get a signal, that they cannot get a meal anywhere at three in the afternoon, or go shopping on Sundays, or flag down a taxi. It's fair to say that it's not everybody's cup of tea, and judging by the numbers of young French people who flee from here to the cities, it's not everyone's glass of *vin rouge* either.

I love the area, but I have to admit that some of my preconceptions about France have been completely shattered. Before coming to live here I always imagined that France was the home of fashion, flair and good taste. Even the words we used in English to describe such matters – sa*voir faire, chic, debonair, suave* – were French. As a schoolboy, I came to believe that France was the source of all things exotic, exciting, adventurous: there was French kissing, French letters, something they called *soixante-neuf*, the Folies Bergère, Pigalle, Brigitte Bardot.

Now that I am older and live in France I see things differently of course. French kissing is no longer a test of how far one can insert one's tongue into somebody else's mouth without making them cough, but has instead become simply a way of greeting people – an unnerving social dilemma which frequently leaves me poised, lips puckered expectantly, only to find that the intended recipient has moved on to eat a sausage roll. In the same way, French letters now take the form of either gas bills or adverts for sit-on lawnmowers. And the *soixante-neuf* position only arises when my wife is searching for the hot water bottle.

Perhaps the biggest surprise is in the absence of *chic*. During my teens, holiday visits to Paris and Nice confirmed my expectations that

French clothes were indeed smarter, French women more alluring (I'm quite sure none of them wore floppy underpants, although I never quite managed to check it out), and French style more glamorous than anything I had seen in England. Mind you, I lived near Darlington, so it's quite possible that a day trip to London, or Oxford – or even Chernobyl – would have had the same effect. No doubt the streets of Marseilles and Paris and St Tropez are still awash with glamorous, trendy, beautiful people. But not here. *Pas du tout!*

By way of example, look at footwear and underwear. The standard footwear around here is not pointy shoes or stilettos or designer trainers. It's wellies and slippers and – would you believe it? – clogs!

A while back I sauntered around our local market, accompanied by my brother-in-law from Chester-le-Street, an extremely pleasant chap – affable, knowledgeable, informative, kind, helpful, infuriating. Malcolm always knows more about everything than I do, and he's six-foot-five and unfairly good looking as well, so I wanted to shake his self-confidence for once by showing him a couple of things that he would never see back in the UK. On the footwear stall I nonchalantly pointed out some *sabots* – French clogs – expecting him to be taken aback, or even flabbergasted. But he was totally unfazed.

"Did you know, Barry," he said in his ever so slightly superior but not quite smug voice, "that our word 'sabotage', and also our phrase 'clogging up the works', are derived from the practice of disgruntled French factory workers in the nineteenth century chucking their *sabots* into the machinery to damage it?" I nodded wisely to confirm that I had been fully aware of this all the time, and tried to vent my irritation by stepping on a passing poodle, but missed. I ask you, how can anybody from Chester-le-Street know things like that?

We walked on through the market and came to the Army Surplus Stall, piled high with all kinds of camouflage clothing and manned by a fearsome looking guy wearing a camouflage T-shirt and muscles. I explained to Malcolm how the French love their camouflage clothing, how all the hunters wear camouflage shirts and pullovers under their mandatory fluorescent orange reflective jackets, and how my neighbour, Monsieur Barreau, even dons a camouflage jacket before he goes out gathering snails. But Malcolm wasn't listening. Instead he stood transfixed, staring – nay, gawping – at a small pile of items priced at one euro each.

I suspect camouflage ex-French army underpants must be something of a rarity in Chester-le-Street, or else Malcolm was trying to work out how some unfortunate soul had had the misfortune to over-estimate how many pairs of camouflage underpants the French army needed and thus generated a surplus. I'd had the same thought myself, and concluded that it's a tricky calculation, because so much depends on what the army happens to be doing at the time. I mean, if you're constantly being attacked by heavily armed lunatic terrorists, I can imagine that your underpant consumption would rise considerably, whereas...

But before I could launch into my theories on the consumption of underpants, Malcolm came out of his trance. "Do people actually buy them?" he asked, his flabber clearly gasted this time. "Oh yes," I replied sadistically, "they're quite fashionable at the moment; in fact, I have a pair that I wear with my labrador pullover."

You see, here in *la France profonde* the French seem no longer to warrant their reputation as classy dressers. I find myself sitting in restaurants alongside ladies wearing galoshes and bobble hats, or

frumpy dresses and white ankle socks. In the supermarket today I saw a grizzled octogenarian with the immortal logo 'Pwer Showr' emblazoned across his red and yellow striped T-shirt. (The 'o' and the 'e' were obscured by his braces). And who buys those enormous, formidable, stiff, flesh-coloured undergarments one sees in some shops? What are they all about?

I think I know the answer. It's because around here they don't care about all the external trappings we British value so much. They want their houses and clothes and underwear to be functional and comfortable and sensible and good value, rather than to impress other people. They actually let their children decorate their Christmas trees, for heaven's sake, instead of buying in the beautiful, perfect, ornate, expensive creations we see in England. Their gardens are used primarily for growing vegetables rather than for looking pretty. They are entirely unimpressed by flash cars or flash jewellery. Or flash gits. I'm sure they would wholeheartedly approve of fur-lined mock-leather balaclavas.

They are, at least in country areas such as ours, just straightforward, unpretentious people with quaint and time-honoured traditions, tastes and customs that have all but disappeared in England: shaking hands, wishing people good day, growing vegetables, chopping wood, killing small animals.

I think they've got it right.

Off my trolley

I CAME TO LIVE IN FRANCE IN PART to avoid stress. I am, you see, a pretty stressed-out individual. I suppose it's because I'm a worrier; I worry about everything and everybody in the world. I worry about how much I worry.

To give you an idea of just how neurotic I've become, let me share with you my latest anxiety. It's that I might not get to the toilet in time. I have no good reason to worry about this: I haven't (yet) had any 'accidents' and I'm probably as continent (is that the word?) as the next man. But as my parents used to say, "You never know" and "You can't be too careful" – either of these could have been our family motto.

So as a safeguard, in the same way that while I'm still two miles from home I take my keys from my pocket ready to open the door, I've started preparing for the toilet well in advance. This latest idiosyncrasy has led to me sometimes actually unbuttoning my fly even before I'm at the toilet door. In fact, on one occasion my wife had to point out to me that I was 'fully prepared', as it were, while still leaving the living room. That takes a bit of explaining when you're at a party.

I impose deadlines on myself for all sorts of things, quite unnecessarily. In the car I have to try and get to my destination before the arrival time predicted by my SatNav. And in the toilet (again) I play the game I've invented called 'Beat the flush', wherein I flush the toilet as soon as I start to wee, and then try desperately to finish before the flush has finished. My wife thinks this is a bit odd – scary even – but I'm convinced that most blokes play this same game, only they daren't admit it.

By the same token I need to be ready, for anything and everything, in good time. I cannot tolerate anything that might hold me up and cause me to miss one of my self-imposed deadlines. So perhaps it's not surprising that I find French supermarket checkouts a major source of stress, second only to Charles Aznavoice, TV adverts for price comparison websites, and the word 'gusset'.

I'm sure I'm not the only one who seethes inwardly, and sometimes outwardly, when stuck behind someone at the '10 items or less' checkout who has the effrontery to unload on the counter eleven items or more. What possesses these people? Are they mad, or innumerate, or just plain lazy? And why do they always get just in front of me in the queue? And why am I the only one to grass them up to the check-out staff? And why do the check-out staff then let them get away with it? And why, for that matter, do other people in the queue then stare at me when I loudly count out the items as they take them from their basket, as though I were the crazy one? Eh? One chap in front of me in the Nontron *supermarché* actually offered the excuse that his six bottles of water should count as only one item because they were all fastened together. Hah! Pathetic! In another life I want to come back as a checkout girl with a big club.

Almost as infuriating are the people who, having waited in front of me for an hour and three-quarters for their turn to arrive, then get a shock when it does. Only when every single item has been rung through the till and carefully packaged into their plastic bags do they remember that they will have to pay, and start a panic-filled search for their purse. And after finally locating the said purse, they then proceed to try to accumulate the precise amount to hand to the cashier. And because these crazy people are probably still working in francs, it follows that they, like the British, cannot count in euros, so it takes them another twelve minutes to assemble exactly eighty-seven miserable centimes in order to avoid giving the cashier a fifty euro note for a bill of 49.87. Meanwhile, I am hopping in agony from one foot to another, clenching my fists and trying hard not to scream.

Then there are the cerebrally challenged customers who forget to weigh their fruit and vegetables, and have to scuttle back to the scales while I moan and keen gently to myself. And what about the items that don't have a bar code, so that the checkout girl has to summon a colleague to saunter casually over to the shelves to track down the offending goods and determine a price? Or the checkout girls who answer the bloody phone in the middle of serving you? Because the phone cannot be kept waiting. It is Technology; it is more important than a mere customer.

Supermarket shopping shouldn't be like this. If only people would be organised and thoughtful, like me, the whole thing could be a pleasant experience for everyone. When my wife first decided that I should do the weekly shop I planned it like a military exercise. After all, I'd run a school, hadn't I? And gained a football referee's certificate (second class). And very nearly passed my Advanced Motorist's test? What could be so hard about shopping, provided one approached it logically and with due forethought?

So first I toured the local supermarket, Intermarché, row by row over a couple of days, noting down which of our regular purchases were located in each aisle. I then turned this data into a computer-generated list showing all the aisles in order, and underneath each of them a list of items to be found in it. Having created this list, it was then but a matter of minutes for my wife to tick the items we wanted.

Armed with my three-page printout I arrived for my first shopping venture full of confidence. I had even brought a clipboard to carry my master list, which I managed eventually to tie to the trolley with a piece of wire, and although it stuck out at the side at an odd angle I could still read it providing I leaned well to my right. Inevitably, this arrangement led to a few difficulties at first, including an almost head-on collision with a rather large French gentleman with no sense of humour, but I soon got the hang of it and, leaning heavily to port, propelled my trolley to Aisle 1.

There, sure enough, lay the tomatoes we needed, closely followed by the lettuce and - right on cue - the apples. My system was surely vindicated, and as I sped past other shoppers I felt a mounting excitement. On to Aisle 2, and with hardly a pause I plucked from the shelves some toothpaste, a pack of toilet rolls and a loofah. We didn't actually need the loofah; I'd been aiming for a pumice stone but my hand slipped, and I didn't want to lose the considerable trolley speed I'd built up.

In Aisle 3 a security guard gave me a long look after I stared at my list and said in what I now realise was an overly loud and triumphant voice, "Straight on to Aisle 4!"

As it turned out, Aisle 6 was my undoing. By now I was virtually running along with my trolley, impervious to the sarcastic comments and startled cries of other shoppers, and as I reached the jars of Bonne Maman jam, exactly where I'd anticipated them, I reached out a nonchalant hand as I sped past. But suddenly, a Dutch child emerged from nowhere and jumped right under my trolley wheels. I knew he was Dutch because he said something like "Ahhgharcjchkowowaadjdjdjschkl" as the jar of strawberry jam exploded on his forehead.

I'll say one thing about French jam: it certainly spreads well. The Dutch boy, all the contents of my trolley and a large section of Aisle 6 were covered in what looked horribly like blood. People gasped, someone even screamed. Somewhat painfully (because by now I'd been leaning over to my right for about twenty minutes) I straightened up, summoned all my dignity, wiped a blob of strawberry jam from my eyebrow, and abandoning both the trolley and the Dutch youth, strode purposefully towards the exit. Without a backward glance I marched confidently through the '10 items or less' checkout (there was only one of me), through the automatic doors, and – breaking into a sprint – reached the safety of my car.

Not surprisingly, I've since started shopping at a different supermarket, where inevitably everything's in a different place. So I started re-doing my master list, only to find that they keep moving things about from week to week. So the Werthers Originals that last week were beside the check-out are this week hidden away in the Sweets aisle between the Snickers bars and the Lindt chocolate. And gouda cheese slices have been transported from the cheese counter into a fridge. The toilet rolls have been integrated with the kitchen rolls, and – how perverse is this – porridge oats has entirely disappeared and been substituted by something revolting called Chocapic.

Inevitably, while I'm struggling to come to terms with all these changes, my shopping expeditions take much longer, so that I sometimes need to break away to go to the toilet. Which raises the distinct and terrifying prospect that one day soon I might find myself 'fully prepared' while in the Tinned Foods aisle.

Oh, the stress of it all...

Mistress required

MOST PEOPLE AGREE THAT IT IS important for British residents in France to integrate into the French community and lifestyle. The alternative – that they stay separate, mix only with their compatriots and cling to familiar customs and lifestyles – does not go down well with the French and throws into question their motives for coming to live here.

Personally, I am all for integration. I'm more than willing to swap my warm half of bitter for an ice-cold lager, Marks and Spencer for Galeries Lafayette, and my goose-pimples for a suntan. I want to be able to speak French fluently, join local associations, grow vegetables, drive a 2CV, and shrug nonchalantly. I will abandon all things British: curries, Chinese takeaways, bowler hats, bulldogs, Boris Johnson, Morris dancing, driving on the left, watching Strictly Come Dancing. Yes, there will be have to be sacrifices – not least finding substitutes for fish and chips and fun-packed weekends in Whitley Bay – but these will be hugely outweighed by the benefits. In this quest, therefore, I intend to mould myself, as it were, on a typical Frenchman.

Which brings me to the rather delicate subject of mistresses.

I have always been led to believe that virtually all French men have a mistress, or several if they are politicians. Why else would French florists, on Valentine's Day, offer two bouquets of roses for the price of one? Well, I suppose everyone needs a hobby, and if you don't play cricket, adultery seems a reasonable, if less exciting, alternative.

Of course, I don't know for sure; it might just be one of those silly stereotypes that attach to particular nationalities, like saying that Scots are mean, hah hah! But to be safe, and in the interests of breaking down cross-cultural barriers, I have reluctantly come to the conclusion that it is probably better that I have one. A mistress, that is. It's not that I want one, you understand, it's just a question of 'when in France...'

But here's the problem: I don't seem to be able to find one. As far as I can tell, there isn't a mistress stall on Piégut market, the local telephone directory's yellow pages jump inexplicably from *maisons de retraite* (old people's homes) to *manicuristes* without mention of *maîtresses*, and an advert I displayed on the supermarket notice board in St Mathieu attracted no serious responses, merely an offer from a young French lady to tutor me in the ways of the world – as if I were interested in geography.

No, mistresses are, to say the least, elusive. I have even taken to leaving my shoelaces unfastened and my face unshaven, on the assumption that prospective mistresses may be looking for a chap who looks as though he isn't adequately cared for. And sometimes when I see an unattached female, I sidle up to her and fix her with what I like to call my James Bond look – you know, the rather cruel, crooked, manly smile and slightly closed eyes.

But would you believe it, I've had no success whatsoever, except that one Dutch lady did ask me if I was unwell. I'm reminded of the tale of the guy who, in an effort to brush up his mistress-attracting skills, ordered from Amazon a book with the intriguing title How to Hug, only to be sent the fourth volume of the Encyclopaedia Britannica.

Perhaps there are none left. Maybe all these insatiable Frenchmen have exhausted, if you'll pardon the expression, the country's supply of mistresses. I hope not. Anyway, I have decided to place an advert in the local paper. There is a section there with adverts for things like old tractors, forthcoming tea-dances and 'memorable happy finish massage', whatever that may be. Yes, I know I am taking a risk, and I'm aware that the flood of responses will possibly clog up the local postal system, but you don't make an omelette without cracking a few eggs, do you?

Of course Kath doesn't understand. In fact she's said she'd die if I ever took a mistress. So I'm thinking of an advert something along these lines:

> MISTRESS WANTED. Mature British journalist of international repute and chest hair seeks a lady/woman for companionship and/or memorable happy finish massage. Ability to organise funerals an advantage.

Things that go squeak
in the night

IT SEEMS THAT EVERY BRITISH person I meet in France is in the process of renovating a house. The men all wear baseball caps and plaster-covered clothing and talk knowingly about unfathomable subjects like zinc guttering, and foil-backed joint binding tape, and non-permeable membranes, and even their partners often seem to be willing and knowledgeable participants. I swear the lady across the road must be knitting a bungalow. Everyone seems to have a project involving the use of concrete mixers or theodolites or, at the very least, basic common sense.

Well, I may as well come clean. I am not Handy. I am not Practical. I cannot Do It Myself. To misquote Sir Winston Churchill, give me the job and I'll finish the tools.

And living as I do in an old French farmhouse, there are forever new problems which emerge to highlight my inadequacies. I have fixed the leaking tap once and for all on several occasions. Last month I tried to seal a gap between wall and floorboards with expanding polysomething foam, which promptly expanded to occupy half the room and seal my right nostril for a good two hours. I have destroyed dozens of those bits that you put in the end of your drill – what do you call them? Ah yes, 'bits' – in a vain attempt to make a small hole in a three-foot-thick granite wall. My friends look disbelievingly at what I like to call my tool-kit and observe that there are only two classes of tools – totally unused or completely buggered.

My incompetence extends to embrace even straightforward, everyday things such as mending a fuse or dealing with God's creatures. Such as mice.

In truth, we haven't actually seen the mice, so we can't be sure what they are like or how many there are. All we've seen are what look suspiciously like mice droppings on the kitchen floor. They must be mice droppings, because no human beings can do poos that small (I know, I've tried).

So I went out and bought two sorts of mouse killer. One sort, cleverly called Souricide (*souris* is French for mouse), comes in the form of teabag things which contain cyanide instead of tea. The other sort takes the form of bars of what looks like soap but is really a deadly poison that will kill anything that moves. So I put these delicacies on the floor before going to bed, and next morning guess what? They'd vanished. No, not the mice – the cyanide teabags and the bars of poison!

Now this was a bit worrying, because it meant that either there was a whole army of mice who somehow managed between them to nudge poisonous teabags and large bars of 'soap' back to their nest, which seemed unlikely, or else – and this is the scary bit – there was just one huge mouse with jaws big enough to accommodate bars of soap and teabags. What's more, this Supermouse, or rat, or puma, or whatever it was, obviously lunched on cyanide. Mind you, we're a bit more opti-

mistic now because the mouse/rat/elephant droppings have turned
yellow. Whatever it is, I may not have killed it, but at least I've upset
its digestion.

I went back to the supermarket a few days ago to replenish my
stock of Souricide, and happened to notice on the shelf some other
interesting products. Between the mouse poison and the bin bags were
all manner of items for seriously inconveniencing all kinds of
creatures. Sprays to deter cats and dogs from coming onto your land,
tiny landmines to blow up moles, potions to poison snakes, kill
spiders, eradicate hornets and flies, sonic alarms to frighten owls and
loirs (edible dormice – don't ask), traps for foxes and for *coypu* (sort

of big rats that can swim). It was all a bit unnerving, I must say.

And here's another thing. Why, in rural France, don't you see any dead birds? There are millions of birds around here, so by the law of averages a few thousand must die every day, but apart from the odd road-kill you don't see any bird corpses lying around. Surely, the foxes can't eat them all? And if they do, what eats the dead foxes? And the dead badgers? And the dead rats and snakes and wild boar? Don't blame it on insects, because by the law of averages a proportion of these aforementioned animals must have died very recently, some within the last few minutes. No time for the insects to have consumed them. Yet they have almost instantly disappeared.

I don't wish to sound alarmist, but I think I'll start locking my bedroom door at night.

Except the lock's broken...

Anyway, back to the mice. Despite my liberal use of weapons of mass destruction, they are still with us. Except for one. You see, in desperation I finally resorted to mousetraps. Kath wasn't too happy, but I reassured her that the end would be instantaneous and therefore painless, and besides, it or they had had enough of chomping their way through of sponges and cloths and were now making inroads into her precious Marigold rubber gloves. So she relented, providing I promised that I would remove any corpses before she saw them.

I actually set four traps, baited variously with two different flavours of cheese, a piece of chocolate and a sugar lump. A bit of a scatter-gun approach, I know, but I reasoned that this way I could see which was their favourite. Nothing happened for a couple of nights, except that I ate the chocolate. On the third night, Kath had invited a few of 'the girls', as they euphemistically call themselves, for supper and I was banished to the local bar to let them get on with whatever it is that women get on with on these occasions.

Apparently – or so a tearful wife explained to me on my return – they had just been discussing the size of Marion's bottom when they heard, from the kitchen, a sort of sharp thwack. Kath knew instantly what had happened, and explained to the others, and they all immediately shrieked and stood up and flapped about. Eventually, the bravest of them – Joyce – was despatched to investigate what had happened. A silence fell while she disappeared into the kitchen, followed by a bloodcurdling scream. The intrepid Joyce came back into the room, looking pale and shocked. "Well, was there a mouse?" everyone asked. "Er no," whispered Joyce, stifling a sob, "just... just a little paw."

Later, I tried to lighten the mood by telling my joke about the cowboy mouse who rode into town and said to the sheriff: "I'm looking for the man who shot my paw," and I even did a rather clever impersonation of a limping rodent, but to no avail.

Mousetraps are out. Souricide, cyanide and the mice are back.

False friends

THERE ARE SOME WORDS IN French that are so similar to their equivalents in English that translation is straightforward, even for a Northerner like me. For instance, I have no trouble decoding a whole host of words ending in 'tion'; *éducation* becomes 'education', *complication* means 'complication', *prononciation* translates as 'pronunciation' (though it's pronounced differently), and so on. Similarly, *adresse* turns effortlessly into 'address', *six* is 'six', and an *ambulance* is still an 'ambulance'.

With so many 'friendly' words around, everyone starts off with a French vocabulary of nearly two thousand words. *Stop* means 'stop', *danger* means 'danger'... you see, you can speak French and you didn't know it! *Extraordinaire*, don't you think? Your *vocabulaire* is already quite respectable; it's not as *compliqué* as you thought. Add to this the French words that have found their way into English usage – *café, croissant, chauffeur, décor, entrepreneur* – and those English words that the French have adopted – weekend, pub, jogging, parking – and you might think that it's all too easy to be bilingual.

Au contraire, Rodney; I'm afraid there are pitfalls – 'false friends'

that look the same in both languages but have different meanings in each. Why, for instance, are the French so awkward and devious as to call a 'bus' a *car*. (Or why, I hear a Frenchman ask, are the English so awkward and devious as to call a *car* a 'bus'?) In the same way, a *crayon* isn't a crayon but a pencil, *location* means rental, an *occasion* is a sale, *monnaie* is just coinage, not money in general, a string in France is always a *thong*, a *decade* is ten days, not ten years, and a *trombone* is a paper clip. Yes, I said a paper clip.

The confusion caused by words which sound the same but mean different things can be excruciatingly embarrassing. My wife once had the misfortune to ask a friend: *"Mettez-vous les préservatifs dans la confiture?"* only to discover later that she'd asked if her friend put condoms in her jam. But there is a town in South West France called Condom, so I suppose for us to call the thing a condom is about as sensible as them calling it after an English town. "Do nut panneek, chérie, I aff brott a Cheeping Norton wiss me."

Similarly, crisps are *chips* ('sheeps') and chips are *frites.* A *mille* isn't a million but a thousand, and *raisins* are grapes. If you're an artist don't stage an *exhibition* because people will expect you're going to expose yourself, and will be disappointed, or relieved, when they realise it's just an *exposition.*

There are more subtle traps, as well. I was in my local bar talking to the *patron* (owner), and I asked, with my usual aplomb, utilising beautiful French intonation, for a *café au lait.* "Ah, you mean a *grand crème,*" he replied. Apparently that's the way to order a white coffee in France; a *café au lait* singles you out as a tourist, whereas 'a big cream please' will impress them.

But don't be afraid to *expérimenter,* and if you want to do the *shopping* and buy your *fiancée* a *bouquet* and then take her to a nice *restaurant* for an *omelette,* well that would be really cool.

As they say in France.

Location, location

WHY, I WONDER, DO SO MANY people who are fabulously rich choose to live in such awful places? Why do they endure the suffocating heat of the Spanish costas, or the madness that is London, or the vulgarity of Las Vegas, when they could live for a fraction of the cost in a tranquil haven of rural bliss, surrounded by gentle rolling hills and gentle people, and insulated from the rush and crush of the twenty-first century?

Here in the Limousin we are far from any huge metropolis, sheltered from the complexities and commercialism of modern life, estranged from the cut and thrust of politics and economics, a million miles from Bluewater, or Wall Mart, or even Marks and Spencer. We can try to keep up with current affairs, but it is rather like reading about dreadful goings-on on some far distant planet, or watching a blue movie: it's vaguely interesting in an academic sort of way, but it's not real life. We have our own planet, thank you, and we are content with it.

To give you an idea of what passes for newsworthy around here, our local newspaper carried a photo last week of a road in St Mathieu that is about to be resurfaced. Wow! And to illustrate how go-ahead and progressive we are, in our hamlet of three houses, we have just been allocated house numbers. Monsieur Barreau and Madame Lascaux were so excited they phoned all their friends to announce the news.

Of course we have all the modern entertainments, albeit in an amateurish sort of way: at the tiny cinema in nearby Nontron there is a sign explaining that films will only be shown if more than five people attend, and this 'big-screen complex', as the tourist information centre refers to it, is manned – or rather womanned – by just one lady, who is ticket-seller, projectionist, manageress and caretaker all in one. If you needed more evidence that we are in a time warp, in Gueret's high street there is to this day a road sign warning horsemen not to gallop.

So we're backward and old-fashioned and out of touch. And glad of it. Life is simple and unsophisticated. It's not perfect: I have to confess that winters, though usually short, can be *triste* (gloomy). Villages can seem deserted, the weather can be cold. People feel disinclined to travel to the large towns and cities for entertainment, and are instead thrown back on their own resources. Families tend to retire behind their closed shutters each evening and do whatever the French do behind closed shutters. Everything slows down, days are short, and rural France goes into semi-hibernation. It would be a good time to invade, if any country felt so inclined; the French mightn't even notice.

But then sometime in March everybody is reborn. Temperatures start to climb, the days lengthen, everything starts to grow, and there is a feeling of anticipation in the air, for we know that in all probability a lovely spring and summer and autumn are in prospect. By the middle of May, every café and every bar is bedecked with geraniums; outdoor restaurants and *boules* pitches and souvenir shops appear as if by magic; the river launch at Brantôme emerges newly-painted to ply its trade and transport white-kneed tourists for a few enchanting miles up and down shaded, willow-lined banks of oleander and lavend... Oh sorry, I seem to have slipped into Peter Mayle mode.

And then we're into the *fête* season, when every town and village has to find a cause, however unlikely, to celebrate. So we have the *fête des cêpes* (mushrooms) in Cussac competing with the *soirée des sardinades* (yes honestly – an evening of sardines) in neighbouring Augignac, and then the next day it's over to Nontron for the Carnaval des Soufflets (Bellows Festival) where the locals dress up in nightshirts, cotton caps, clogs and masks and try to blow their bellows up ladies' skirts. Oh what fun! When I asked them why they did this, the answer was: "Because it is the only day they will let us do it." Serves me right for asking.

Meanwhile, there is the annual *vide grenier* (loft sale – the equivalent of a car boot sale) at Pensol, and a few kilometres away Maisonnais is staging a village barbecue and dance featuring the awesome Ladyboys Rocking Group backed up by Sinister Misshun.

There is virtually nothing that the French won't celebrate. There are chestnut fairs, wood fairs, cider days, beer festivals, wine festivals, flower festivals, gourmet days... all of them an excuse for the villagers to sell their wares, share a slap-up meal, drink too much wine, gossip, joke, sing, dance, and generally make merry: days filled with simple, unsophisticated pleasures, full of *bonhomie* and *camaraderie*.

Of course there are national *fête* days as well: Bastille Day,

Armistice Day, Labour Day, Victory Day, Assumption, Ascension, Epiphany, Pentecost, Crêpe Day (honestly), Music Day, La Toussaint (a day to honour deceased relatives), Mothers' Day, Valentine's Day, April Fool's Day, Mardi Gras... the list seems endless.

And what about this: if you are a metal worker, you get an extra day off – the holiday of St Eloi in July. I asked a neighbour why metal workers were so special. "They are special because they specialise in work with metal" was the reply, which left me feeling a bit silly.

One of my favourites is the first of May each year, the Fête des Muguets (lilies of the valley) – an occasion to give little posies of these flowers to your friends as a token of your affection. So smitten was my wife by this tradition that when she happened to meet some friends in a supermarket on the day in question she searched the shop to find a little bunch of lilies of the valley, and when she met them again, in the frozen foods section, she proudly presented the posy with an embarrassed little speech about how much she valued their friendship. It was only later that evening that it suddenly dawned on her that they would have had to pay for them at the check-out!

They took it well, but now if we meet them while shopping I have to keep checking that they haven't smuggled a television set into our trolley.

Of course, there wouldn't be time to enjoy all these *fêtes* properly without a few strikes here and there. So throughout the summer groups of workers impatiently await their turn to go on strike. No-one strikes in the winter, for that would mean suddenly having some spare time to paint the house or mend the fence. But in summer a carefully organised week of industrial action inevitably means long afternoons spent drinking pastis in the shade of a plane tree, or sweaty, indolent games of *boules*, or gentle promenades with the family, lugging enormous picnics and life-sustaining bottles of wine.

My friend Jean-Paul explained to me that the co-ordination of these strikes is vitally important. "Eef the lurry men wonn to mekk jems on the mutterway, they must be sure the farmers are nut ollreddy mekking jems wit their tracturs, or their lurries would not get there. And eef we wonn to mekk the strake, we must nut mekk it on a day of *fête* – thet would be to shoot ourselfs on the legs."

And on top of the strikes there are the *manifestations*, or demon-strations. Our friend Monsieur Coussit solemnly declined our offer of *aperitifs* last week with the immortal words: "I em desolated to refuse, but you see I ev to manifest myself in Angoulême."

Yes of course this is a backward and unsophisticated region. But I want to live in a village where the English papers arrive two days late. When I first came to live here I asked at the local *tabac* if they sold English papers. "Yes off course," came the reply. "Do you wonn today's pepper or yesterday's pepper?"

Somewhat taken aback, I said: "Well, today's please."

"Then you must come back tomurrow," came the impassive reply.

And I want to have neighbours like old Monsieur Barreau, who invites me to go round at midnight so we can sit in his garden and listen to a nightingale and drink a chestnut liqueur or six. I want to live among people who wear slippers to go shopping, who will expect and value a five-minute chat at the check-out, who distrust plastic money, whose national sport is tax avoidance, who drive bad cars badly, and who cling to old-fashioned values.

I love being wished a *bonne après midi* (good afternoon), a good appetite *(bon appétit)*, and in the same vein a good Wednesday, a good end of the week, good luck with whatever I happen to be doing (*bonne continuation*), or even the French equivalent of 'best of British luck!' – *bon courage!* I love it too when I walk into the bakers and everyone turns to say hello. I want to be able to pee at the roadside, drink a glass of *rosé* for breakfast, spend two hours eating lunch, have inefficient log fire heating, gather wild berries, go to tea dances, and have endless discussions about my *fosse septique* (septic tank).

And how's this for nice? We sometimes come home to find that someone has left us a present of home-grown tomatoes, or perhaps a marrow, in a bag they have hung on our gate – a neighbourly offering made for no particular reason other than kindness.

Or how's this for quaint? All our neighbours plant their vegetables according to the phases of the moon. My initial reaction was to think that the poor old souls knew no better, but now I'm minded to believe they must be right, because they are wise beyond measure about surviving and thriving in a rural environment. They find mushrooms where none should exist, their hens produce more eggs than seems feasible, their tomatoes ripen long before mine, their stoves burn better, their flowers are more abundant, and they can foretell the weather with uncanny accuracy. (Monsieur Barreau has, hanging on his front door, a sort of withered cactus which he uses – don't ask me how – to predict when it is going to rain. Me, I follow the Météo France forecast on the television. Guess which of us gets wet?)

California may have the weather, Paris the culture, St Tropez the *chic*, and Switzerland the scenery. But for me they don't have the allure of quaintness – the charm of a chestnut fair, or the timeless grace of gentle people.

Of course it can't last. Already there is a McDonald's in Limoges,

the first hoodie has been spotted in St Junien, and rumour has it that there is a man in Rochechouart who can nearly use an iPad. We are on borrowed time, I'm afraid. Progress is head-butting its way remorselessly towards us, and one day soon we will have wi-fi and Starbucks, the mayor's 2CV will sport personalised number plates, and Wayne Rooney will build a holiday château outside Montbrun.

Ah well, enough of that. It's a sparkling Tuesday afternoon in May, all's well with the world, and I think my *Sunday Times* might be in.

The anomalous behaviour of water in the nought to four degrees celsius range

HAVE YOU NOTICED THAT WHEN it's really hot we British still tend to talk in terms of degrees Fahrenheit: "Whew, it's in the nineties." Then on bitterly cold days we revert to Celsius and complain that it's minus two or minus six, rather than say: "Brrr, it's twenty-eight outside."

I suppose this ambivalence reflects our attitude to Europe in general. After eleven years in France I still haven't come to terms with expressing my car's fuel consumption the French way, in litres per hundred kilometres. Instead, I go through a convoluted mathematical conversion exercise to change it into good old mpg. And all so that I can boast that the little C3 gets 612 miles to the gallon (maths was never my strong point).

Similarly, my wife tells me I embarrass her in our local supermarket by staring at the carrots and chanting in a stage whisper: "Two and a quarter pounds of jam weighs about a kilogram," or else examining a bottle of fruit juice and solemnly reciting: "A litre of water's a pint and three-quarters." I suppose anyone listening would deduce, correctly, that I am either an ex-teacher or a nutter. Or both.

But back to temperature. My brother-in-law Malcolm has been staying with us. He is a scientist – a physicist, no less – and therefore extremely knowledgeable about How Things Work. It was Malcolm who many years ago diagnosed the fault on my Mini as a cracked vermiculite shroud, and Malcolm who explained to me, over the course of a fortnight, Why We Have Sunsets. You know what I mean. Malcolm is Wikipedia on legs, without the need for independent citations.

By bitter experience I have learned, when in his company, not to ask any questions which might give rise to a Malcolmian answer. If I want to know why water freezes, or why smoke rises, or why planes fly, I prefer to ask my wife, who in her role as an infants teacher was often confronted by such queries. She would simply retort: "It's just magic." This always seemed to satisfy her five year olds, and of course it meant she didn't have to learn National Curriculum Science. A generation of schoolchildren in County Durham have thus grown into adults who believe devoutly in the supernatural, mysticism and Paul Daniels.

But I slipped up the other day. Malcolm and I were enjoying a beer on the patio, and even though it was February it was a beautiful day with warm sunshine and a steely blue sky. I glanced at the thermometer on the patio and casually remarked: "Heavens, look at that: middle of February and it's sixty-eight degrees!"

I knew instantly that I'd blundered. Malcolm was out of his seat in a trice and staring at my thermometer, a maniacal, scientific gleam in his eye. "No it's not," he said triumphantly. I cringed. I was going to pay dearly for my slip. "You see, Barry, your thermometer is in direct sunlight, and so it's experiencing an effect called diathermancy – known to the man in the street as the greenhouse effect."

"Yes of course," I interjected in a Midas-like attempt to stem the impending tide of scientific information. "How about another beer?"

But Malcolm had started and he was going to finish. I was obviously one of those men in the street, and needed to be shown the error of my ways. "You see, infra-red radiation from the sun is short wavelength because it comes from a high temperature source: the surface temperature of the sun is approximately six thousand degrees centigrade." Here he paused for dramatic effect, and by way of an aside threw in: "The core temperature, incidentally, is thought to be between fourteen and twenty million degrees Centigrade, which is how it can maintain the fusion reaction between nuclei of the hydrogen

63

isotopes denterium and tritium, which is the process by which all stars produce their heat and light."

I stared, fascinated, at two lizards copulating, or arm-wrestling – it's difficult to tell with lizards – in the warm/hot/boiling February sunshine.

"Short wavelength IR (yes I'll have another beer, thanks) can pass through the glass bulb of your thermometer, raising the temperature of the thermometric liquid, which is probably an alcohol stained with red dye because water would be no good due to its anomalous behaviour in the nought to four degrees Celsius range."

I wondered about diverting him towards the reproductive system of lizards, or kicking him in the groin, but thought better of it (he's six-foot-five, and even taller in centimetres). And then I contemplated maybe feigning a seizure, but too late: Malcolm was well into his Patrick Moore mode. "So the alcohol is now warmer than the ambient temperature." He looked at me as if expecting a response, and I was just about to mumble something about vermiculite shrouds when he resumed. "So it tries to radiate IR to those cooler surroundings."

Can you believe it? The bloody lizards were at it again, but this time there were three of them, and it didn't look like arm-wrestling to me.

"And because the alcohol is a low temperature source, it radiates long wavelength IR which doesn't pass so well through the glass as short wavelength IR; so the temperature of the alcohol trapped within the glass enclosure rises."

What would John Cleese have done? Pass out? Die? Set about Malcolm with the branch of a tree?

By now my brother-in-law was warming, if you'll forgive the pun, to his task. "In consequence, the temperature of the alcohol trapped within the glass enclosure rises." Yes, I'd noticed my beer was getting warmer. But by now the whole conversation had become somewhat pointless, because the sun had set and it was getting decidedly chilly.

Just then, my wife appeared with her sister. "Now what have you men been talking about?"

"Well," I volunteered, "Malcolm's just explained why our thermometer isn't accurate."

"Oh, why is that then?"

Like Lionel Messi pouncing on a loose pass, Malcolm was on topic and in his stride. "Well you see Kath, your thermometer is in direct sunlight and..."

I managed to change my scream into a sort of friendly chuckle. "I think what Malcolm means, Kath, is that it's magic."

The lizard

FRANCE CAN BE DANGEROUS. IT'S not just the mice, and the bees and wasps and hornets, and the motorists, and huge buzzing insects, and heatwaves, and snakes, and wild boar, and estate agents. Most of these can be coped with (except, perhaps, estate agents). But what is really difficult to cope with is the unknown: the things that rustle and scuttle and lurch about in the dead of night.

Let me explain. Last night, my wife and I went to bed. I was feeling, how shall we say, a trifle amorous (dangerous enough in itself at my age), and fortified with a couple of pre-nuptial whiskies I was lying there, puzzling over how I might counter whatever arguments my wife might advance against my evil plans. Because she is good at that. Over forty-something years of marriage she has long since moved on from the prosaic "Sorry, I've got a headache" and invented a whole range of what I have come to call Reasons For Not. They include: "No, I haven't had a shower," "No, you haven't had a shower," "Not when I've just had a shower," "So that's why you've been grinning like a simpleton all night," and recently the priceless "Sorry, I can't stop thinking about the subjunctive."

Nevertheless, a few minutes later all seemed to be going well, when suddenly Kath sat bolt upright and screamed. Not a scream of rapture, you understand, just an ordinary, straightforward, everyday scream. "There's something in here!" she gasped. Unsure at first of what she meant, I thought of continuing my endeavours, but it was not to be. "Listen, there's something breathing!" I listened. Nothing.

"It's something, I tell you. It's moving. It's alive. It's watching us. KILL IT."

Sighing, I switched on the light, and there, sure enough, peering at us from the foot of the bed, was a tiny lizard. It was a beautiful little thing: smooth, sleek, green, perfect. Now I know my wife, and I knew instantly that any ambitions I might harbour would never be achieved with the lizard around.

Have you ever tried to catch a lizard? In the middle of the night? In the bedroom? In the nude? Let me tell you, they're bloody fast. My fly swat proved useless, as did my pillow and my left slipper. The lizard simply gave me the run-around. And just when I felt I'd got it cornered, by lying on my side and making my outstretched body form the hypotenuse of a triangle between two walls of the room – a trifle undignified but damned clever, I thought – it cheated, and ran straight up the wall. There it sat, upside down on a roof beam, smirking nonchalantly at me.

Rising to the challenge, I stood somewhat precariously on the bed and tried to swat it with a copy of *Le Figaro*. I must have come close, because it skittered across the ceiling, down the opposite wall and into my half-open sock drawer. I inched forward, fly-swat poised, sweating slightly, humming the theme tune from *Where Eagles Dare*, and with lightning reflexes slammed shut the drawer.

I returned triumphantly and hopefully to bed, but Kath was not placated. "You can't just leave it in there. What happens when you need to get your socks out?"

"Well actually, I've been thinking that perhaps I'd give up wearing socks. Lots of these French guys don't seem to bother, and you've always said my ankles are my best feature."

"But you can't just leave a bloody lizard in your socks drawer for ever, you fool. What about the smell?"

I misunderstood. "Oh, it'll get used to the smell."

No use. The lizard and Kath spent an undisturbed night in their respective beds, and I took to thinking about how dangerous France is.

And about the subjunctive.

Twitch your way through France

WELL, I'VE BECOME AN EXPERT at something at last.

Back in England my knowledge of birds was limited. Oh I knew a hen when I saw one, and a budgie, and probably an owl, but that was about it. The vast majority I classified simply as Little Brown Jobs or Big Grey Jobs. Oh sorry, I also learnt how to recognise a pheasant, after I squashed one.

But out here in rural France, the place is fairly teeming with birds. Birds of every size, shape and colour. You see enormous great things with claws and teeth, that might actually be eagles if they aren't buzzards or kites or vultures, watching you hungrily as they perch on fence posts, licking their, er, beaks. And huge cormoranty things that could just as easily be storks or flamingos or cranes... or pterodactyls, for all I know.

I went for a walk with a twitcher the other day. Now just in case you're thinking I should choose my friends more wisely, let me explain that a twitcher is the common name for a bird-watcher. And just in case you're still thinking I should choose my friends more wisely, let me explain that the birds in question are the feathered variety.

Anyway, he clearly knew his stuff, and he kept up a constant stream of excited whisperings as we stole furtively along the lane behind our house. "Over there," he would whisper, "Eurasian Thick-knee!" then "Good Lord, a Ruddy Turnstone, I do believe," and later "Shhh; Little Bustard," which upset me for a while. I was enormously impressed, I can tell you, and I determined there and then to become proficient at bird recognition.

To start, I thought I would compile a list of all the birds I already knew, and frankly I surprised myself. Alongside robins and owls, I listed exotic things like emus, ostriches, parrots, penguins, geese and swans. But let's face it, you're unlikely to encounter an emu or a penguin in France, so that wasn't too helpful. No, I needed to be able to pick out woodpeckers and kingfishers and nightingales and blue-bearded minch dwellers, and the other ornithological occupants of the forests of the Dordogne.

So I bought myself a bird book. *Birds of Europe: a Spotter's Guide* it said. Huh! Now don't get me wrong: the book was beautifully illustrated and extremely informative. Each page explained in great detail the characteristics of every bird and – importantly – their distinguishing features.

So I learnt that in order to differentiate, for example, between a stone curlew and a Senegal parrot, you should be aware that the latter has less yellow on its bill. And although the short-toed treecreeper has toes the same length as the normal treecreeper, which is a bit of a disappointment, it is nonetheless a bit smaller. Oh this was exciting! How impressed were people going to be when I nonchalantly pointed out that what they supposed was a tree pipit was in fact a meadow pipit, by virtue of its longer hind claw.

But as I read on it became clear that twitching was going to be a little trickier than I had imagined. Did you know, for instance, that the thing which differentiates the long eared owl from the short eared owl is not ear-length – it's eye-colour? Yes, eye-colour! I can just imagine the sadistic lunatic who discovered this species slapping his thighs and shouting joyously: "I've got it, Henry. We'll call the one with the grey eyes the Long-eared Owl."

What's more, even if you learn all the different characteristics, it seems you still can't always be sure. I quote: 'A long-legged brown bird with a markedly down-curved bill... may be either a curlew or whimbrel, or even a slender-billed curlew.' So that's all right then.

Undeterred, out I went in search of creatures with short toes, long beaks, thick knees, yellow tails, curved claws, and so on.

But what the book didn't tell me was how to find these damn birds and persuade them to sit still long enough and close enough for me to find their picture in the bird book. Not much chance of examining a pipit's hind claw when it's whizzing past in a blur of feathers at eighty miles an hour, or of checking whether that distant dot eleven hundred feet up in the sky is a tawny eagle or a spotted eagle.

I did actually find something with thick knees and strange markings on its breast, but it turned out to be a boy scout.

And even when the birds were reasonably co-operative and let me get within seven miles of them, the differences between them were so insignificant that you would need to examine them under anaesthetic with a magnifying glass to tell them apart.

So how can I describe myself as an expert, you might ask. Well, expertise is relative, is it not? And though I may not know as much about birds as David Bellamy, I know some people who know less than me. This is very important in life. If you always mix with people less clever than yourself, you can always appear relatively clever, see? Watch Gary Lineker.

Oh, you should see me now when some of my townie friends come over from England to stay. They come from places like Middlesbrough and Darlington, and are therefore babes in arms when it comes to bird recognition. The nearest they ever get to a bird is eating a McChicken sandwich or watching porn.

So I have great fun taking them for a walk, then stopping suddenly to examine a small pile of poo on the ground and saying something like: "Hmmm, there's been a wilch-gobbler here, and it looks like it's been eating grass seed again." Or "Hear that? Gosh, if I'm not mistaken that was the mating cry of the Granfrew's tit, just out of earshot."

One of my favourite ploys is to suddenly stop, look worried, cast furtive glances about, and say quietly: "Don't do anything sudden; just stay very close to me and try not to breathe for a few minutes; it's probably nothing more than a dark chanting goshawk, but best not to take chances." I then take out my trusty Swiss Army knife and grimly flex my ankles. It seldom fails.

Those emus had better keep out of my way.

Nonplussed in France

'NONPLUSSED' IS A STRANGE SORT of word, don't you think? I mean, one never speaks of being 'plussed', so how can one possibly be nonplussed?

If that opening sentence has taken you aback and left you puzzled and unsure of how to respond, then I've probably nonplussed you. But never mind. The point of this bizarre introduction is that I find that, living in France as I do, I am frequently nonplussed by all sorts of things. Only last week I had an extremely nonplussing experience.

I was driving my wife's Citroen C3, on my way to the market at Piégut in response to her command to look for "some of those little ceramic things that you rest your knife and fork on between courses when you have French people to dinner because they expect to keep their cutlery from one course to the next", and working out what the appropriate sign-language might be. I saw the road sign warning of loose gravel, but I always ignore such warning signs ever since I slowed for a Beware, Cattle Crossing sign in 1986 only to find there weren't any cattle anywhere.

But this 'loose gravel' warning turned out to be for real, with the result that I lost control of the car and smashed into the metal railings on one side of a bridge.

I was unhurt, but the car and the bridge looked like they'd done a couple of rounds with Mike Tyson. In fact the car dangled on its side from what was left of the bridge and threatened to fall into the small beck beneath. I wondered briefly about re-entering it to try and salvage my Werthers Originals from the glove compartment, but thought better of it. Fortunately, a friend – a British ex-policeman – lived just half a mile away, and a quick call on my mobile phone brought him to my aid. I was a bit shaken, so I was happy to go along with all his suggestions: "Think of a good excuse or they'll do you for careless driving," "Phone your insurance company," "Phone your wife," "Phone the police," "Stop dithering," and so on.

While we waited for the police and recovery truck to arrive, I concocted what I thought was a very plausible excuse. Just as I had neared the bridge, a huge bird – almost certainly an eagle – had swooped in front of the car, and at the same time a deer had leapt in front of me. In a desperate attempt to preserve French wildlife, I had courageously and selflessly swerved the car into the bridge, endangering my own life in the process.

But while I was trying to work out how to say all that in French, a small crowd materialised from nowhere and gathered by the wreckage. It was as if they'd all been hiding there, just waiting for the day an Englishman crashed his car. There were three or four local farmers, along with their wives and a couple of goats, a passing cyclist, and a French family who decided to abandon their car trip to wherever in order to join in the general merriment.

Inevitably, as time passed, the French onlookers became more and more vociferous and animated. A bottle of wine appeared from somewhere and was passed round. Not a lot happens in these parts, and this was probably their most exciting day since the Germans left. The ambience became increasingly good-natured and boisterous, and I half expected them to start an impromptu barbecue or a tea dance.

Eventually, one of the old farmers asked if I had phoned Monsieur le Maire to tell him the bad news about his bridge, and I had to confess that I hadn't thought of that, but by way of atoning for this oversight I mentioned that I had called the police. "The poleece?" asked the old guy in an incredulous voice. "But non, you must not hef coll thee poleece. Thet is a foolish ting." The other onlookers nodded in agreement, and muttered gravely among themselves, shaking their heads and clicking their teeth, and generally looking worried and disapproving. "The poleece weel com and you weel 'av to blur in the beg," said the farmer.

But the police were charming. Instead of arresting me or shooting me, they actually called me "Monsieur" and even shook my hand, which nonplussed me even more. Having thus softened me up, they then became business-like and – sure enough – made me blur in the beg. They seemed surprised and a tad disappointed when the result proved negative. After a quick look at my tyres (not difficult because two of them were at eye level) and some more handshaking, they departed, leaving me to await the breakdown truck and the humiliation of having to tell my wife of her car's fate.

"Honestly, Kath, this bloody great eagle just came out of nowhere..."

As soon as the police had gone, the crowd broke into excited chatter, and eventually one of them approached me and said: "Monsieur, we are all wondering, what eppen when you blur in the beg?"

"Well, nothing," I replied. "*Nègatif.*"

"But Monsieur, it is three in the afternoon."

"Yes I know. Would you believe I've been here since before noon."

He looked at me incredulously, then turned and translated this news to his compatriots in rapid and excited French. There was much oohing and aahing, and a few "*Mon Dieus*". Even the goats looked surprised.

It took a few moments for me to grasp what they were thinking: it was the middle of the afternoon and this strange Englishman was perfectly sober. The poor man must have completely missed lunch. *Quelle horreur!* How can one possibly function without three courses and a *pichet* of wine?

No wonder he had managed to lose control of his car and demolish a bridge.

I think I had nonplussed them.

Lyin' Air

(your no-frills, low-cost, no-comfort airline)

THANK YOU FOR USING LYIN'AIR's new internet flight booking service. Please retain the following flight confirmation details, which you must present on check-in:

Reservation Code LA 1661HT

2 return seats Liverpool to Limoges

Outward Departure Time from Liverpool: 3.12 am

Return Departure Time from Limoges: 3.40 am

To finalise your booking and help us to tailor our service to your specific needs, please answer these simple questions:

Do you wish to purchase a LYIN'AIR hand luggage bag at only £99? Note that these bags are specially designed to fit snugly into our ever-popular LYIN'AIR hand luggage cages at the airport, which in turn are specially designed to be just an inch or two smaller than nearly all other makes of cabin luggage. **YES/NO**

If not, why not? ....

Unfortunately, for safety reasons, we are unable to allow passengers to carry with them anything which we deem to be dangerous to other passengers or to our profit margins. These include anything even remotely edible, drinks of any kind and in any quantity, handbags, children, medical items (including heart pills and inhalers, dentures, hearing aids, walking sticks, contact lenses and surgical stockings), knives, books, shoes, coats, newspapers and socks. Note that, in line with our Customer Service Policy, heart pills and inhalers will be available during your flight from our cabin crew at our special LYIN'AIR prices, along with an endless procession of scratch cards and the communal copy of last month's in-flight magazine, *Cheap-o*.

We have formed a lucrative association with Formula Con Hotels and can honestly say that you won't have stayed at any hotels as cheap as these. Please follow this link – www.formulacon.com – and indicate which hotel(s) you would like to stay at and for how long.

- ❑ Please tick the box if you do not wish to purchase a LYIN'AIR loofah at only £6.50. A great gift for the grandchildren and a wonderful memento of your journey with us.
- ❑ Tick the box if you do not want to buy an amazing almost-guaranteed-to-win LYIN'AIR scratch card at £2 (or 5 for only £12).

Elsewhere, cunningly hidden among a long list of inappropriate options, you may be able to locate a box for you to tick if you do not want to take out LYIN'AIR travel insurance.

In the event of sudden depressurisation, those passengers who have subscribed to LYIN'AIR's Breatheasy option (£40 supplement) will have oxygen masks drop down in front of them. In addition, those who have taken out our Superbreatheasy policy (£60 supplement) will find that their masks actually have oxygen coming out of them. Please tick the relevant box(es).

❏ Gosh yes, I'd like to register for Breatheasy

❏ Never mind that, put me down for Superbreatheasy

❏ I'm not one to take chances with my health; I'll have both

❏ Tick this box if you are absolutely sure you do not want travel insurance.

We have negotiated a special, mutually beneficial car-hire arrangement with HiringHurtz at only £60 a day (all-inclusive) for a reliable pre-owned Robin Reliant van with opening windows and space for a radio. Please specify if you do not wish to avail yourself of this facility and instead use dirty and overcrowded public transport. **YES/NO**

Travel insurance is strongly recommended in case we lose your luggage again or in case your plane plummets blazing into the ground somewhere over Normandy. Should that happen, with our specially negotiated insurance deal LYIN'AIR will pay for your full funeral costs providing you apply in person at the check-in desk at what would have been your destination.

❏ Tick the box if you are still determined to be a prat and not take out insurance.

If using HiringHurtz (all-inclusive) car-hire, do you wish to take out supplementary insurance (only £50 a day) to safeguard you against paying an exorbitant excess should you damage, dirty or even smudge the hire car? **YES/NO**

Do you want to be chauffeur driven to and from the airport by one of our liveried serfs? (Price on application). Please note that for a small supplement we can arrange for you to be driven very slowly past your neighbours' houses. **YES/NO**

If you really insist on taking luggage with you, we can offer a special reduction of 20% on our normal £140 a case (up to 6 kilos), for anyone using a LYIN'AIR suitcase, available for only £300 by ticking this box: ❑

What about travel insurance? Eh? **YES/YES/YES/YES/NO/YES/YES**

Priority boarding is really a must nowadays – in fact with LYIN'AIR it is a must. So popular was the scheme with our passengers that last year just over 50% of our clients opted for Priority Boarding and the chance to get on the plane before lesser passengers. We have therefore extended the scheme, and have become the first low-cost carrier to have compulsory priority boarding for all passengers, at a cost of only £20 per person! This development means that no-one need feel left out or intimidated by their fellow-fliers, and is in line with LYIN'AIR's equal opportunities policies. Next year we will begin trialling our innovative Priority Priority Boarding scheme, whereby for an additional £40 better-class clients can be given priority over all the Priority Boarding passengers.

If you are intending to bring any musical instrument with you, or to sing or whistle during the flight, please note that for safety reasons we have to make a surcharge of £80 per item or £5 a note. Be advised that we have added an automatic £10 surcharge to all bookings to pay for the stirring musical fanfare played whenever we land safely, or on time, or at all.

Flight punctuality has been somewhat disappointing on the Liverpool-Limoges route, so we are up-rating our estimated flight time for this journey from 2 hours 40 minutes to 6 days. In this way you and we can be assured that LYIN'AIR's enviable reputation for 90% of flights arriving on time is maintained. We aim to bring our entire service up to the standard set by our Gatwick-Alicante route, where we consistently manage to save four hours on a three-hour flight.

Seats next to emergency exits can give you that all-important edge when our planes catch fire and have to be evacuated. If you value your life, or the lives of your loved ones including small defenceless children who trust you implicitly with their well-being, you can secure this valuable advantage for only £40 a seat. Similarly, elderly, frightened or renally-challenged passengers can reserve a seat near (or even inside) the toilet for only £20. And for the same surcharge passengers can reserve aisle seats which permit you to have our attractive stewardesses brush coyly past you. Tick as appropriate:

❏ Emergency exit seat

❏ Seat near toilet

❏ Seat inside toilet

❏ Aisle seat

Turnaround times have now been reduced to an industry-leading 8 minutes. Please leave the plane quickly when we land (it will help if you start to edge your way towards an exit soon after take-off), otherwise we cannot guarantee that you will not still be on the aircraft when it takes off again, or indeed that you will not spend the rest of your days trying vainly to disembark.

Wheelchairs are not tolerated on LYIN'AIR flights; they can all too easily be transformed into armoured personnel carriers and as such constitute a real threat to our wonderful safety record. Besides which, they also tend to contain people who are handicapped, and such clientele is inconsistent with our aims for an eight-minute turnaround and with our Equal Opportunities for Able-bodied Passengers policy.

Please note that a standard £10 surcharge will be applied for all passengers paying by credit card. Note also that payment can only be made by credit card. The one exception is for payment using our special LYIN'AIR credit card*, available for only £120. *(APR 1500%).

This is your last chance for insurance. Non-insured passengers will be required to wear a sign round their neck saying Uninsured Cheapskate, and will inevitably find that their cases have all been routed to Tashkent. Kindly tick the box for our special-deal insurance, and give yourself peace of mind for only £20 a day. ❑

Finally, please be aware we have regrettably had to add an extra surcharge of £15 per passenger to all bookings to compensate for the

European Union's insistence that we offer passengers delayed by more than seven months a free cup of tea.

Thank you for booking with us. Just remember our slogan: How Cheap Can We Get?

And for the love of Mary, Joseph and the Other Feller –

❏ BUY THE FECKN INSURANCE!

Global warming

DURING THE COLDER MONTHS, one of the joys of living in rural France is the smell of wood smoke, as every little cottage in every little hamlet lights its wood-burning stove. And I very much want to be part of this cosy world and to make my own contribution to global warming, and spend whole evenings in front of a roaring fire, drinking whisky and listening to my wife.

But this is assuming that one has a roaring fire, and let me tell you that that is somewhat harder to achieve than the accompanying glass of whisky and gentle diatribe. Permit me to describe for you the fascinating and life-changing process by which wood moves from its pristine, natural, pastoral state to become fuel in one's wood-burning stove. It is a story of devil-may-care heroism and stubborn determination; a tribute to man's extraordinary ability to harness the natural order to his needs.

So first man cuts down trees - very big trees usually - using fearsome snarling chainsaws the like of which you don't see in B&Q. (You can always tell a tree-feller feller: just count the fingers and toes.) These mighty trees are duly sawn up into great logs and loaded onto huge lorries which then tear about the countryside cutting corners, breaking speed limits and eradicating parked cars and startled tourists, in a manner which you can only do if you are driving, or should I say aiming, something which weighs a hundred and twenty-six tons and doesn't belong to you.

Eventually, the logs are deposited at farms or wood-yards, where they are sawn up into one metre lengths. In time, they are bought either by Frenchmen who take them home and split and cut them into smaller pieces using a sharp Stanley knife, or else by woossie expats who pay a fortune to have this done for them. They are then carried by trailer or tractor and dumped a suitably inconvenient distance from one's barn or woodshed, so that one has to wheelbarrow them the remaining distance and stack them into an orderly pile.

But the tree's remarkable journey isn't over yet, because of course the wood has to somehow find its way into your house, indeed into your stove. This is most often achieved by the man of the house wheel-barrowing, over the course of an average winter, what seems like several thousand barrow loads of logs from the barn to the house, invariably in rain or snow, and then bringing them into the house and placing them in some sort of basket, from whence they eventually make their last journey to their funeral pyre.

For some unfortunate men there is an additional step which involves banging the logs together and then brushing them – brushing them! – in order that no sawdust is spilled within the house. As far as I can tell there are only four men in the whole of Europe who are required to perform this intermediary function; needless to say, I am one of them.

And then the pyre has to be lit. Just how difficult this process is depends partly on the sort of wood you have bought and partly on whether you are an arsonist or just an arse. There are, you see, all sorts of different logs – oak, acacia, chestnut, pine, sycamore, ash, beech, and so on. And these different logs all have different, usually feminine, characteristics. Some spit and snarl, some smoulder interestingly, some ignite quickly and burn furiously, while others just lie there, inert and listless, rather like England midfielders.

Me? Well frankly, I can't tell my acacia from my elder, so I'm in trouble straight away. And then the damn logs come in different lengths and diameters, and different sized logs should be placed on different parts of the fire. Oh yes, and if any of the wood is damp on

the inside you're completely lost, but you can't tell if it's damp inside until you try to burn it.

And no self-respecting man would ever stoop so low as to use firelighters; oh deary me no. Instead, they go out into the French undergrowth and collect something called 'kindling', and then they rub two boy scouts together to ignite the kindling, which in turn lights the logs, giving a roaring fire in a few seconds.

I can never locate these kindling trees so I use firelighters. I am not self-respecting.

I'm sure most French people are born with all this knowledge. Many have it in their genes, while others have probably studied the niceties of log fire lighting at the Sorbonne. I've watched them light their own fires, and it's like spontaneous combustion. But for an impractical, useless, self-disrespecting Englishman like me it's just too much, especially when my wife shouts: "Stop throwing so much wood on the fire; it doesn't grow on trees, you know." So I finish up hurling the tongs onto the floor and drinking whisky. I think I was born with the knowledge of how to drink whisky.

Now I cannot be the only person who finds it difficult to light a fire, for that would imply that I am peculiarly and singularly inept. So for the benefit of all those who share my problem, I offer this simple 30-Step Firelighting Guide, based on some ten years of experience in deepest France and a great deal of trial and error.

1   Look for matches.

2   Fail to find matches.

3   Grumble a bit, then tear off piece of kitchen roll, form into taper, and take over to cooker.

4   Attempt to light gas ring on cooker by repeatedly pressing piezo ignition button.

5   Fail to ignite gas ring. Grumble a bit more.

6   Go into barn and change eleven ton gas canister for another eleven ton gas canister.

7   Press piezo ignition button repeatedly and impatiently.

8   Observe piezo ignition button roll across floor. Continue grumbling.

9   Look for matches.

10 Find matchbox containing four matches. French matches. Spindly French matches.

11 Waste first match by striking too hard and causing it to snap in two.

12 Say "Golly Gosh" or words to that effect.

13 Repeat process with second match.

14 Successfully light third match thus allowing burning end to fall off onto cardigan. Fight back tears. Say "Yes, darling, I'm just lighting it now."

15 Successfully light last match and use it to ignite gas ring.

16 Hold kitchen-roll taper over gas ring and ignite it.

17 Endeavour to get back to fireplace before taper burns down to fingers.

18 Fail.   >>>

19 Shout a bit and say "Drat" or even *"Merde"*.

20 Light another taper and this time almost reach fire just as it begins to burn fingers. Drop taper onto rug. Whimper a bit.

21 Abandon kitchen roll, and instead rip end off Weetabix packet and ignite said end on gas ring.

22 Rush to fireplace, standing on piezo ignition button and crunching it into thousand pieces.

23 Use end of Weetabix packet to light firelighter.

24 Put assorted logs on top of firelighter.

25 Watch as flame of firelighter slowly dims and dies.

26 Repeat Steps 19 to 25.

27 Think of trying petrol.

28 Decide against.

29 Turn on central heating.

30 Drink whisky. Get warm, and chill.

Who moved my Q?

WHO WAS IT SAID "LIF'S A BITCH and thn you di?" Wll h, or sh, was right; I cam to Franc for a lss complicqtd lif, and what happns? On on prfctly ordinary Fbruary day, out of th blu, unannouncd, unhraldd, for no apparnt rason, my computr dcids to stop printing th lttr ' '. No mattr how hard, or how oftn, I prss th ky, th ' ' just won't appar; Rally, I could scram.

I suppos thr is som consolation – I can now typ swar words confidnt in th knowldg that thy won't b cnsord – words lik 'buggr' and 'hll'. But what about th bautifully craftd ssay I was about to pn on th Frnch ducation Systm, h? Why dos it always happn to m? With anyon ls, th 'j' ky might hav xpird, or mayb th '+' ky. Wll you can mang without thm, but not th ' ', th most commonly usd lttr of all.

Just as an asid, hav you noticd how asy it is to rad an articl without any lttr ' 's? Maks you think mayb w could do without this lttr altogthr. Think of th mony that would sav: smallr kyboqrds, thinnr books, lowr production costs and thus chapr nwspaprs, chapr road signs, fwr lttrs to rad and writ, so a sving in tim, giving us mor lisur tim. I might just writ to our Prim Ministr and suggst this; it could b a ral vot winnr at th nxt lction. It would also sav m having to gt my wrtchd computr mndd.

So, dar radr, tak a sht (hop you'r rading this right) of papr and s what wird nw words you can mak from xisting words, just by omitting th ' 's. Or try having a convrsation with you partnr whr you omit all the lttr ' 's; Kath and I do this somtims and always nd up in tars of laughtr. Somtims sh narly wts herself! Herself... herself! Eureka – my 'e's back! Oh joy!

Of course I could have just transferred to my other computer, except that it's French and so has a French AZERTY keyboard instead of the more familiar QWERTY layout. Believe me, this makes the task of typing fiendishly difficult. With quite a lot of keys being in the 'wrong' position, one has to search carefully for them.

To give you an idea of what it's like to suddenly have familiar things moved to a different place, imagine that you wake up one morning to find that your nose has been re-located onto the end of your foot, and your big toe has replaced it in the middle of your face. Inevitably, you're going to find yourself for a few weeks absent-mindedly blowing your foot, and at some stage you will quite possibly contract athlete's nostril. Life becomes less predictable and you suddenly wish you'd cut your toenails more often.

It's the same problem that you get when you start to drive a left-hand drive car: you are forever going to the passenger door to get in, and then, to save face, you try to pretend that really you'd gone around to that side on purpose to adjust the rear view mirror. So then of course you have to adjust the bloody mirror to preserve the charade, and then you have to stop later, out of sight of any onlookers, to adjust it back again.

And did you realise that to type a full stop on a French keyboard you have to first press the Shift key, otherwise you get a semi-colon? What kind of nonsense is that? A full stop is one of the most commonly used keys, so why didn't they make it easier to type? I mean, you can't always be ending your sentences with a ; can you?

Just as annoying is that you have to remember to press Shift whenever you type numbers, and if you forget, today's date becomes (:é:é&' instead of the much more sensible 5/2/2013. By the same token, a 9 mutates into a ç and a 0 into an à.

By way of compensation, though, it's a lot easier to add accents to letters. And there are some cute characters, like '§'. Now I've never needed to type '§' before, but it's sort of reassuring to know that I could if I needed to. It's dead easy on a French keyboard. The same goes for ° and ù, and even µ.

Try it and you might learn to love your French keyboard.

Vive la difference!

Driven to distraction

THE FRENCH ARE REPUTED TO be a passionate people: stubborn and determined, proud to be 'citizens' rather than 'subjects', artistic, adventurous, intolerant of petty restrictions. They are ebullient, effervescent, impetuous, irrepressible. They are filled with *élan* and *joie de vivre,* topped up with *vin rouge.*

Not so the British. We tend to be somewhat reserved, cautious, conventional, taciturn. The French say if there's one Englishman at a bus-stop he'll form a queue; we like order, fair play, everything in its place.

Of course these are crude stereotypes, and the longer I live in France the more I realise how much we all have in common. Such differences as there are tend to be superficial and unimportant. We are generally taller than they are; they tend to be thinner than us. They adore Johnny Hallyday, while we prefer mushy peas.

But I want to focus on one important difference; one which could, unless rectified, re-ignite the Hundred Years War. I am talking about the French disposition to tailgate. By which I mean following far too close to the car in front.

Now, for the sake of political correctness let me emphasise that I am not claiming that the British are better drivers. I am sure that the French motorist is at least as skilful and considerate as his British counterpart, except in this one area. And maybe a few others.

When it comes to keeping a safe distance behind the car in front, I'm afraid their driving is, not to put too fine a point on it, *merde*. I don't mean little diddy poo-poo windy-pop *merde*, I mean full blown, no holds barred, in your face, stinking, glutinous, X-factor *merde*. *Merde* with attitude. *Merde* so big you can see it on Google Earth. *Merde* so vast that it has its own postcode.

A Frenchman behind the wheel is in this respect a loose cannon, a wild stallion, a free spirit. A nutter. No matter that he is driving an ancient white Renault van, or a cute little 2CV, or even a tractor. He is the Master of his own Destiny, the Captain of his Ship, the King of the Castle, the Top of the Heap. What's more, you are in his way! You are preventing him from achieving his desired speed, which is precisely 2kph faster than you are going. And you are audaciously occupying the very bit of France that he needs to be in, namely a small section of tarmac two metres in front of his bonnet.

Understandably, given that he is proud, passionate etc (see paragraph 1) he must correct this state of affairs. And to do this, he must first flash his lights at you and sound his horn repeatedly. This warning – the equivalent of a bull pawing the ground – means that if you don't veer out of the way and let him past he will either overtake, or else position himself four feet behind you, unerringly locked on to your rear number plate, umbilically conjoined, until you move over and let him get on with what remains of his life.

Nowhere is this more evident than on the peaceful, winding roads of the Limousin. It seems that every time I venture out in my trusty C3 I am immediately assailed by a French driver whose sole aim in life, or so it seems, is to physically mount my poor little Citroen, and probably its driver as well. The offending vehicle attaches itself with an invisible thread to my rear bumper, and we proceed as if glued together.

Now I'm a reasonable chap, and I've tried all sorts of tactics to persuade my adversary (for such he is) to back off. I've tried winding down my window and shouting something a bit like "Back off!" at him. I've touched my brakes in an effort to frighten him. I've gesticulated via the rear view mirror, utilising the international hand-sign for 'Please keep two car lengths away'. But all to no avail. At best, I get an uncomprehending look of genuine bewilderment, or else a

96

Gallic shrug, or a retaliatory international hand-sign: 'I'm only one metre away from you.' I've thought of paying to have a flashing sign installed in my rear window, so that with one push of a button I can initiate a luminary caution, something like 'I am about to engage reverse,' or 'If you come any closer you'll have to marry me,' or 'Watch it, pal, I'm probably taller than you.'

I'll readily admit that I'm not quite a perfect driver myself, and I'll confess to having in my time written off a Humber Sceptre, a Mini, a sit-on lawnmower and a golf buggy. But none of them through tailgating! Why do they do it, then, eh? *Pourquoi?*

Worst of all, of course, are the lorries. All French lorries seem to be driven by hulking great brutes of men, exceptionally tall for their nationality, and swarthy to boot. So you've got to go a bit steady with the international hand-signs, even if their eighteen-wheeler Norbert Dentressangle pantechnicon is intent on copulating with your modest and virginal *citadine*.

But I find I have a rather more understanding attitude towards these lorry chappies. I tend to forgive them, and rather than hurling insults at them or shaking my fist I just hunker down in my seat a bit and pretend to study my fuel gauge. Oh, I did once give a French lorry driver a rather withering look, but he was going the other way so I felt pretty safe, although I did hop around nervously when I later stopped at an aire, lest he should have exited, changed carriageways and pursued me.

On another occasion I had the temerity to flash a lorry who'd forgotten to dip his headlights, only for him to switch on what appeared to be sixteen sets of runway lights and blind me and all the other drivers within a kilometre! No, my advice is to leave these good fellows, with their beards and stubble and moustaches and muscles and sleeveless vests, and names (displayed proudly in their cabs) like Serge and Hubert, well alone. They're only doing their job. And anyway, they're almost certainly drunk.

Your anger is probably better directed at elderly lady drivers and not very tall war veterans. But you won't stop the French tailgating. I have this theory that they do it, subconsciously, to show other road users what fast reaction times they have. "Look at me, *mon ami*; I ken drive wizzinn 80 sauntimettre off zis eedio in fron' becoss my réaction are 'oned to perfecseeon. Eef 'e should brekk, or even stop, I will be just a blurr of movemon, a well-oiled machine, and wizzinn tree nanosecond weell 'av assessed ze situasseeon, engeged my 'azard wonning lights, geeven a slowing down seegnal, med a couple of phon colls and brott my car to a beautifully controlled 'olt. Off course, we should oll kep a seff deestance be'ind ze car in fron', but what ees *extrêmement dangereuse* for an ordinary mortal ees patetically easy for me. Would you expect Alonso to drive troo Piégut at fifty keelomettre an 'our? No, eet would be an insult to 'im. Did Mark Spitz wear ammbands? Did Superman bozzer weet a crash 'elmet? Ze next sing, you'll be wanting me to wear a seat belt!"

So don't expect French drivers to change. Better to fall back on those British qualities that the rest of the world so admires and stay calm: keep a stiff upper lip, maintain your dignity, turn the other cheek, look both ways and use a condom.

After all, we have our stereotype to maintain.

Five across and three down

ONE OF THE ODD THINGS ABOUT coming to live in France is that you leave all your past behind, and therefore you can, if you so wish, re-invent yourself. And some British people do just that. As they make that final journey across the Channel or through the tunnel they magically mutate into joiners, or plumbers, or estate agents, or computer experts, or whatever. No matter that their entire work experience to date was cleaning graffiti off walls as part of a community service order, they suddenly have the opportunity to describe themselves as tradesmen, or financial advisers, or retired gynaecologists! For who can gainsay them when no-one any longer has any information about their past, and when even their accent fails to give their French neighbours a clue as to their background?

Well, the author isn't like that. Oh no. I haven't pretended to be anything but the hugely intelligent, handsome, urbane, rich, polo-playing Concorde pilot that I was in England. Except for the other day.

I should first explain that I love doing crosswords – notably *The Times* crossword. It's not so much that I actually enjoy the process of solving the clues, but rather that I gain immense satisfaction from nonchalantly throwing down the completed crossword and seeing the awe and admiration in people's eyes. Actually, I only ever successfully completed *The Times* crossword once, and that was in 1986, but people are still impressed if you get only a few clues, because for all they know you've only just started on it.

So what's this got to do with France, I hear you ask. Well, since I came to live in France, amazingly, I have become much better at *The Times* crossword. I have, if you like, re-invented my crossword skills.

It started as I sat at a crowded pavement café in Piégut, drinking my *pastis*, thoughtfully sucking the end of my aviator sunglasses and generally trying to look like a retired Concorde pilot. I had completed three clues in *The Times* crossword, and realised that a somewhat attractive lady was glancing at me, and then down at my paper. She was tall, slim and elegant, with an unmistakably French aura about her, and I could sort of sense that she was imagining me on the polo field.

So I attacked the crossword with a new vigour, and suddenly I had a brainwave. She was French, wasn't she, so how could she possibly know if I was putting in the correct answers? Eureka! Deftly, I filled in 7 Across – 'Traffic warden goes to ground in American state'. Yes of course, CABBAGE fits nicely, doesn't it? Then 3 Down – tricky, this one – five letters ending in G and the clue 'Mood music found in the playground'. No problem. I quickly entered FLIEG. Well, why not? By now I was getting the hang of it, and my hand moved in a rapid blur across the page. No sooner had I glanced at the clues than answers flew from my pen:

SISTER, ENCOURAG, DAR, CRICKETBA, YHUMONG, FRUTUBUTW, CLEVRS... There was just no stopping me. OHOHOHOQ, ROONEY, PERNAXD... I reckon I finished the whole thing in under five minutes,

and triumphantly placed the paper on the table while casting an intelligent, handsome, urbane, rich pilot's glance at my companion.

Slowly, she picked up the paper and looked at the crossword. Then she looked at me, and with eyes full of Gallic intensity, whispered, in an unmistakable Brummie accent, "Ee, yows a sad kise, pal."

I tried to retrieve the situation by using one of my favourite ploys. "Can you help with 12 Across?" I asked innocently. "The clue is 'Postman's sack'."

Her brow furrowed with what passes for concentration in Birmingham. After an eternity she said: "How many letters?"

"It's full of them!" I screamed triumphantly, guffawing and smacking my thighs with glee. "Full of letters, you see... a postman's sack... full of letters!?"

I don't think she was very impressed. Maybe I need to re-invent myself again.

Boules: the roules

I HAD THOUGHT THAT I MIGHT pen an insightful and penetrating article on French taxation law. And then I thought "Balls!" Or rather, since I am refined and live in France, I thought "*Boules*".

So instead of pondering the intricacies of how to fill in an incomprehensible French tax return when I could never fill in an incomprehensible British tax return, I decided instead to offer this Foules Guide to Boules. This is not a treatise for experts or *aficionados*; instead, it aims to present the basic rules and niceties of the game in a way that will help British residents or holidaymakers to join in without making total fools of themselves as quickly as usual. So let's begin.

Boules is a game played by Frenchmen with very heavy balls. Consequently, very little activity is required – I mean, if you've got heavy balls you don't want to be swimming, or horse riding, or, perish the thought, hurdling, do you? No, *boules* is a gentle, non-strenuous and extremely simple game. Teams consist of one, two or three players. In teams of three, players use two balls each, while in teams of one or two they use three balls each. The only other equipment needed is a measuring tape and an ample supply of alcohol, preferably *pastis*. Now, wasn't that easy? Stay with me, because there's more.

Following a brief argument, one team throws the *cochonnet* (a very small ball, about the size of a – well, a small ball, actually) a distance of between six and ten metres. This seemingly straightforward task usually proves impossible for the British, who invariably throw it a number of yards by mistake, and always too far or not far enough. If that happens, you may choose either to kick it a bit further forward or backward, or else re-throw it, or else just brazen it out.

The team that throws the *cochonnet* throws their first ball and tries to get it as close to the *cochonnet* as possible. The other team then does the same. The team that ends up further from the *cochonnet* then throws again, and continues to throw until they either use up all their balls or throw one which lands closest to the *cochonnet*, at which point the other team gets to throw. Thus, whichever team is closest to the *cochonnet* at any one time simply watches and makes rude comments and sips alcohol while the other team throws. Within a team, the players may choose whose turn it is to throw. They may take alternate throws, or one player may throw two or all of his balls before the other throws.

Now this is where it gets a bit tough, so please concentrate. When all the balls have been thrown, the team which is closest to the *cochonnet* scores one point for each ball they have closer to the *cochonnet* than the closest of their opponents' balls. Read this again and again until you understand it. Ask your partner to read it out to you. Try writing it out a few times. Or listen to it on tape each time you go out in the car. It is not that difficult; most people catch on after only a few months.

Players then have an obligatory drink of *pastis*, and the winning team gets to throw the *cochonnet* for the next 'end'. This process is repeated until one team reaches the winning total of thirteen points, or until all players are too drunk to care. At which point everyone retires for several more obligatory drinks.

And that, really, is it. But anyone who wishes to take the game seriously – God forbid – should be aware that there are many more rules designed to cover every possible contingency. For instance your balls should really have their weight stamped on them, though British players seem curiously averse to this delightful custom and have sometimes to be physically held down to have it done. Moreover, your balls must not have any foreign bodies attached to them (just picture it!) Tampering with another chap's balls is strictly forbidden. However, deliberately smashing your own ball into one of your opponents', though it might seem extremely un-British, is a perfectly legitimate tactic to the French, who tend to play *boules* like they drive their cars.

Ladies, of course, do not usually have their own balls (except for those who come from Middlesbrough), and so must use those of either their husband or a close friend. And ladies are generally discouraged from participating in *boules* matches in case they make fools of themselves, or – worse – win.

It may be helpful for potential players to be aware of some of the more common utterances which are employed during games. Chief among these are *"Catastrophe!"* meaning "Oh what a dreadful shot," (or, for Northerners, "Bugger!") and its converse *"Bien joué"*, meaning "What a brave and incisive shot my opponent has just played," (or, for Northerners, "Lucky bastard!") Then there is *"Ooh la la!"* meaning "I say, I have just played a remarkably good shot, don't you think?" (or, for Northerners, "That'll teach you to fart in church!") If you are feeling generous, you might say "*Elle est belle,*" meaning "Gracious, but that was a telling shot, and one which has left your team closest to the jack," (the Northern equivalent being "Gerrootathat hinny!" which the French have no end of trouble with).

Finally, a few tricks of the trade, or dubious tactics to which a true Brit would never resort. Clashing one's balls together loudly just as an opponent is about to throw is considered to be the worst sort of gamesmanship, and is agonisingly painful to boot. And clashing one's opponent's balls together can be fun, but it is hardly in the spirit of *entente cordiale.* Ostentatiously cleaning or polishing one's balls with a soft cloth is allowed, and can prove a useful distraction; it is also immensely comforting on a hot day.

And one final tip: all men know that coughing makes your balls retract. Therefore, if you think you have launched your ball with too much vigour, a paroxysm of coughing during its flight may on occasion slow it up and prevent an overshoot. It is important to prevent an overshoot, especially in mixed doubles

So there you have it. The Good Boules Guide. And I must say it has served us well in our local expat Boules Group, somewhat ambitiously called Total Boules. We meet every Tuesday morning at the Bar Feuillardiers in Marval, and spend the first hour or so innocently chatting. This is the only time the seventeen blokes involved meet up without our wives, and so it affords us a rare opportunity to talk men's talk – you know what I mean: politics and literature and art galleries and opera and suchlike, and just very occasionally a little football and cricket and cars and motor bikes and, er, well, other male interests.

Then after a couple of beers we draw lots for teams and wander

twenty metres to the *boules* pitches just behind the bar. We must make an impressive sight. For a start, we all dress very differently. There is no dress code for *boules*, so in an effort to look suitably athletic we each wear something from our distant sporting past. David wears trainers, Stuart a rather nifty baseball cap, Kevin a figure-hugging T-shirt which shows off his fine physique (the bastard), and Malcolm a pair of shorts reminiscent of the Raj. I am content to wear a rather up-market golf glove with cut-out back and knuckle holes and stud fastener closure, while Richard is resplendent in his motorcycle leathers and an Aussie rain hat. I think Richard has problems.

And if our attire doesn't set us aside, then our unique throwing styles certainly do. There's Geoff, who for some reason is physiologically unable to chuck a *boule* without – illegally – lifting one foot from the ground and pirouetting round until he is almost facing backwards, a bit like a Russian hammer thrower. And then, after releasing his *boule*, he contorts his body in a vain attempt to modify its trajectory, an exercise which always makes him look ridiculous, like some septuagenarian rap dancer, and which occasionally leads to him actually falling over. And even then, lying on his side in the dirt, he will feebly flap an arm to show his *boule* which direction it must take.

Malcolm has devised his own trademark shot, catapulting the *boule*, underarm, at a fearsome speed towards the unsuspecting *cochonnet* or an unsuspecting ankle. Malcolm can fairly be said to lack finesse. Malcolm is what we term a tosser.

Then there's Robert, who always seems to think he is launching a mortar as his *boule* flies to a ridiculous height while everyone runs about and ducks and yells "Incoming!" And Mike is famed for his unusual and slightly off-putting bottom-wiggle as he winds up to unleash his missile. Meantime, Little Phil, who takes things seriously, is desperately entreating Archie to concentrate, while Archie is far more interested in making sure no-one is drinking his *pastis*.

And all the while we exchange insults, and accuse each other of cheating, and have seething arguments and tell dreadful jokes at each others' expense. The French cannot understand how we can be so rude to each other and still remain friends, and still less can they fathom why we insist on playing on virtually every Tuesday of the year, come hail, rain, or even - honestly - snow. They shrug and nod knowingly at each other and mutter *"Ils sont fous, ces Anglais!"* (They are mad, these English).

And of course they are right.

Whistle a happy tune

MY WIFE CAN'T WHISTLE. THAT'S not a criticism of her. It's simply a dispassionate, totally non-judgmental observation, like saying she can't speak Serbo-Croat, or pump iron, or fly. It doesn't mean she's not a totally wonderful and talented person in absolutely every other conceivable respect. No, not at all. So I hope that's clear. Dear.

But while she's aware that she can't speak Serbo-Croat, and is almost convinced she can't fly, for some reason thinks she can whistle. So she does. And I'm not criticising her in the slightest, you understand.

The trouble is, whenever she whistles, it makes me want to wee! No matter that I've just been to the toilet a few minutes ago and haven't had a drink for several weeks, just one tiny trill is enough to get me going. In the waterworks department, that is.

And here's the bad part. She has become aware of the effect her whistling has on me and is using it to make my life very difficult. She deliberately waits for the most inconvenient moment – just as I'm dozing off to sleep, or watching England take a vital penalty, or nearing the front of a very long queue at Carrefour – and then launches into the shrill wheezing screech that is her version of whistling. Just so she can watch the result. I'm not even safe in church: the other week she decided in an evil moment to quietly whistle the third verse of *Onward Christian Soldiers*.

Most annoying of all is when I'm driving. And this brings me to the point of this article. I live in France, so why should it matter if I need suddenly to have a wee on the outskirts of Périgueux, or at the traffic lights in Nontron? I can just do what the French do and wee nonchalantly at the side of the road.

Except it isn't as easy as that. In the first place, being a man, I find I have to wee against something. It is a well-known fact that men cannot wee directly onto the ground. Instead, we must find an object – a tree, a urinal, a passing bee, a traffic warden, whatever – so that we can wee against the side of it. I don't know why; it just is.

So the first problem, if you're a man, is that you have to move away

from the safety of the car and find a discarded bicycle or some such item. And even when you've done that, it's still not easy. Because another well-known fact is that British men cannot wee in public. The French make it look easy, I know, but take it from me, if I am to find some relief from the whistling-induced agony that Kath inflicts on me, I have to be unobserved.

Now that's all right if there's a convenient bar handy, or a tent, or – best of all – a cave. But can you find a cave when you want one? So instead you have to go into the undergrowth. (Thankfully, living in the Limousin, there is nearly always some undergrowth to go into. What would I do in Liverpool?) But not too far into the undergrowth, for the deeper into undergrowth one goes, the more dangers that lurk.

Now I'm not a sissy, and I once nearly shouted at a skinhead, but let's face it: when you're alone in the undergrowth in a foreign land, and when you're at your most defenceless because your, er, your... vulnerability is exposed, as it were, you are suddenly intensely aware of all the potential dangers that lurk and scuttle around you in the undergrowth. So I find myself looking around furtively for anything that might bite or sting or – perish the thought – chew: wasps, or ants, or spiders, or snakes. Snakes – God help us!

All of these would be frightening enough if one encountered them while dressed in a full diving suit, but when one is in one's shorts and shirtsleeves, with one hand already spoken for, and with the most fragile of flesh invitingly exposed, it is a terrifying ordeal. I even need to keep glancing nervously skywards in case a passing heron should be hovering patiently above me, waiting for the right moment to skewer its dinner. Aaaaargh! Can you imagine it? Having your whatsit mistaken for a stickleback?

So you cannot afford to relax. And then, as you well know, the moment you have begun, and the steam is slowly rising to encircle you, it is absolutely inevitable that a car will come past. Or more likely a bus. And always carrying a load of jeering ladies clutching binoculars.

This happened to me just the other day, but I was ready for it. Normally, I would simply have bowed my head and pretended that what I was really doing was trying to read a very small map. But this time, as they sped past, gawking and tittering at my embarrassment and leering and shouting out of the windows, I decided to show them how nonchalant and urbane and man-of-the-world I was, and – I waved back!

A mistake.

It is impossible to wave while at the same time looking out for wild boar and ferrets and squirrels (think about it), and yet manage to keep the rest of your body completely still. If you ever contemplate this manoeuvre, take my advice and wear waders.

And the next time you see a Frenchman nonchalantly relieving himself at the side of the road while simultaneously eating a *croissant* and winding his watch, show him some proper respect. 'Cos it ain't easy!

Incidentally, my wife has just pointed out that women don't have it easy either. Apparently, as they squat there in the undergrowth they are even more vulnerable than we men, for in addition to all the dangers that threaten us, they have to keep an eye out for nettles. And hedgehogs, for God's sake!

The mind boggles.

No more Mr Nice Guy

The Moving Finger writes; and, having writ,
Moves on; nor all your Piety nor Wit
Shall lure it back to cancel half a Line,
Nor all your Tears wash out a Word of it.
— *The Rubaiyat of Omar Khayyam*

I HAVE ALWAYS TRIED NOT TO offend anyone with the stories I write. Oh, I poke gentle fun at a few people, especially myself, but it's all rather safe and anodyne.

Well, as I write this it's New Year and since Santa didn't bring me what I asked for I've resolved that things are going to change. No more gentle sideswipes. No more subtle nuances. No more euphemisms. No more Mr Nice Guy.

Instead, my writing is going to become a source of biting and incisive social comment, and the bites and incisions are starting today! I intend to take up the sword of freedom (perhaps my Swiss Army knife will have to do) and brandish it with courage and tenacity. I shall speak my mind freely and without thought to political correctness. I shall tackle head-on those very issues which are the most provocative and controversial. In short, I am going to rant. Just watch me. I will become one of Europe's most feared and respected journalists, a sort of French Jeremy Paxman but with a bit of Anne Robinson thrown in for added vitriol.

But where to start? Frankly, there are so many things to rant about that it's difficult to choose. There's international terrorism, for instance, which is generally reckoned to be A Bad Thing and therefore an inviting target for my scathing wit and devastating criticism. Then there's those dreadful French *8 à huit* shops which mysteriously only open from 10 to 4. Or perhaps I should have a go at Angela Merkel, or smokers, or those lunatics who erect dangly Father Christmases on their chimneys and then LEAVE THEM UP UNTIL LATE AUGUST. Oh yes, there's going to be a lot of capital letters, mark my words.

And just to start things off I'm going to turn the searching spotlight of international investigative journalism on British people living in France. That should quickly earn me a goodly number of enemies and establish me as a Writer Who Knows No Fear.

Now let me say at the outset that I have nothing against most of the Brits living in France – I'm one of them after all, and so is my charming and intelligent wife who is also beautiful and doesn't look fat in her new jeans and who is peering over my shoulder even as I write this. But honestly, some of them! Within a ten-kilometre radius of where I live there can be found expats who have never attempted to learn a word of French, refuse to eat French food, have been arrested and imprisoned for growing cannabis, work 'on the black' (thereby taking work from the French who work on the black), and for all I know sleep in their vests, wear Union Jack underpants, are called Jed and support Chelsea.

You'll see that I've tried to temper some of my searing criticism with a little humour, but not enough, I hope, to mask the sincerity of my antipathy towards those of my compatriots who, in my judgment, let the rest of us down by showing us up. Most French people encounter only a limited number of British people, and inevitably they are going to formulate their opinions on the basis of this restricted experience, so there is a responsibility – nay, a duty! – on us to be good ambassadors for our nation.

In fact, I feel so strongly about this that I reckon there ought to be a new criminal offence, somewhere in terms of seriousness between treason and parking without lights, called Bringing One's Country into Disrepute. Those found guilty of this offence – and that would include all those listed above, together with all English football hooligans and anyone who has ever worn a knotted handkerchief on their head – should be instantly deported, preferably to Middlesbrough, and have their passports and/or their genitalia confiscated and burned. Perhaps a limb or two might be amputated at the same time, *pour encourager les autres.* France, and the world in general, and maybe even Middlesbrough, would be a better place for it.

But, I hear you ask, who would police such a system? Who would make the judgment as to whether a particular behaviour was likely to Bring One's Country into Disrepute?

It would need to be someone with extraordinarily good taste, impeccable character, delicate judgment and unimpeachable credentials. Someone who was NOT AFRAID TO SPEAK, OR WRITE, THE TRUTH. I think you see where I am going. Yes, as someone who has never knowingly had his credentials impeached or his character pecced, I would gladly volunteer myself for the job. In fact, if M Hollande could be persuaded to issue me with a Kalashnikov and an unlimited supply of ammunition, and of course a licence to kill, I am confident that in a few years I could rid France of all the English pond life, riff-raff, failed genetic experiments and general undesirables.

I would probably start by driving round in my Humvee and shooting all those who were wearing baseball caps the wrong way around, and those I caught walking around France with no shirt on. I'd then take out anyone who wore socks with their open-toed sandals or who wore a nose ring.

Of course, there would inevitably be a few innocent casualties – I might not be able to distinguish between a gormless work-shy alcoholic and a retired educational psychologist until it was too late, and I suppose I could easily mistake an ex-tax inspector for a feckless lout. But they would die in the knowledge that their demise was for the greater good.

Maybe there would need to be an alternative punishment, somewhat less harsh, for a few. After all, being blown away might seem a tad severe for someone whose crime was to Come from Essex or Wear a Cravat. Maybe it would suffice to make them live on one of the Spanish costas, or in Afghanistan.

Well, what do you think? As you've probably gathered, I'm really a softie liberal at heart, so I'm quite prepared to listen if you think there are any other offences which would constitute Bringing One's Country into Disrepute, or any more fitting punishments for the guilty, or even any other groups you would like me to have a go at in future essays (nuns, perhaps, or estate agents?)

I realize that I have now made myself a target for all those whom I have offended in this article, including most English football supporters and everyone from Benidorm, Chelsea, Essex or Middlesbrough. I suppose I am most at risk from the reader (and there must be one) who works on the black, wears Union Jack underpants and likes the odd joint. And if he happens to be called Jed, then I'm a dead man.

But the Moving Finger Writes...

Le soleil

MY DAUGHTER LYNDSAY IS A sun-worshipper, and when she and her partner Dave decided last year to holiday in Provençe she was anxious that the two of them should be able to sunbathe. But Dave has ginger hair and a freckled complexion, and burns at the slightest exposure to the sun's rays. My wife worries inordinately about him when he comes to visit us in France. On one occasion she insisted he apply Factor 10 sun-cream on top of Factor 5, "because 15 is so much safer".

So just before their expedition to Provençe, Lyndsay despatched him to their doctor with instructions to find some sort of preparation that would allow him to spend time in the sun. The doctor duly obliged with a special cream. Not a conventional sun cream, you understand, but a very medical and greasy and smelly and above all expensive lotion which he assured Dave would give him absolute protection from any amount of ultraviolet rays providing he applied it liberally.

Arriving in St Rémy de Provençe, they hired a car and set off for a run. Dave was plastered with the special cream. It was a very hot, sunny day, and he drove with the window open, smoking a cigarette. It was the open window that was his undoing, for suddenly the wind blew the glowing end off his cigarette, and to his horror it landed on his forearm and there it stuck to the cream, and actually set it alight! With Lyndsay screaming, and his arm literally on fire, poor Dave managed to steer the car off the road and into a lay-by.

To their amazement (and you really have to imagine what were the chances of this happening) they were followed off the road by a police car, and an agitated *gendarme* ran to them with a fire extinguisher and proceeded to spray Dave's arm and extinguish the flames.

This story would have been incredible enough if it had ended there. But there was more to come. For just as Dave was recovering his composure and stuttering his thanks, the policeman booked him. Yes, really!

I suppose there are several threads to be drawn from this story. Beware the Provençal sun. Don't smoke and drive. Be thankful for the French police, but at the same time don't assume that they are soft.

Oh, by the way, I didn't mention what he booked him for.

It was possession of a firearm...

Christmas crackers

THE FRENCH DO CHRISTMAS differently from us. For a start, their Christmas season runs from around mid-November until early January, whereas in the UK it seems to last from April to March. And it's far less commercialised in France, although there are ominous signs that this can't last.

It's the eighth of November as I write this, and the local *pompiers* (firemen) have just called to 'give' me my free calendar, for which they expect a Christmassy donation to their funds. I'm very happy to do this, because they carefully note down each donation, and there is a rumour that if you summon them in an emergency, they first consult their donations list.

Soon, we'll receive further free calendars from the postman, the rubbish collectors, the local football club, and so on. So I've no excuse for forgetting my wife's birthday next year.

Some of the French Christmas traditions are similar to ours. Many families still come together to attend midnight mass *(messe de minuit)* on Christmas Eve, and afterwards they have their traditional Christmas dinner, *le reveillon*, which starts sometime after midnight and finishes often at around four in the morning. Before retiring, the children leave their shoes by the fire so that Santa (Père Noël) can fill them with sweets and trinkets.

They make a special Christmas cake, as well: in the past, it was traditional to keep a log burning in the fireplace from Christmas Eve until New Years Day, but that particular tradition has been replaced by the creation and consumption of – would you believe it? – a delicious cake in the shape of a log, the *bouche de Noël*. The French don't miss an opportunity to eat well.

But a couple of traditions we don't share. Our French friends are amazed at our custom of sending – at great expense – Christmas greeting cards to everyone we know, even to people living in the same house. The lady in our local post office throws up her hands in horror as yet another *rosbif* comes in to buy 146 stamps.

And they don't understand our passion for Christmas crackers. I was trying the other day to explain the concept to some French friends, who grew ever more incredulous at what they clearly thought was an entirely pointless and foolish British tradition – rather like cricket, or queuing, or invading other countries.

"And then you each pull one end until the cracker snaps – yes, that's right, you sort of tear it in half. Ha ha! I don't know why. If you're lucky, one of the cracker-pullers will fall off the chair and slightly injure himself. And then there is a bang and... What? Well, a bang is a sort of small explosion. Some sort of gunpowder I suppose. G-u-n-p-o-w-d-e-r. It's, er, an explosive. Not really dynamite, and no, certainly not Semtex. Nothing as bad as that. Just a very small amount. Hardly an explosion at all really, more like a quick bang. Stop laughing, Kath. A bang, I said. BANG. It's onomatopaeic. Sorry, the

French word for onomatopaeic escapes me for the moment. It's just BANG, for God's sake! Come on, you must have bangs in France. I know, it's like a sort of loud POUFF! You do have pouffs in France, don't you? Of course I'm being serious. And then a worthless trinket falls out, something along the lines of a tiny plastic dinosaur, or maybe a little balloon, together with, um, a hat. I'm afraid I don't know why a hat. Well you put it on your head, of course. It is made of paper. Yes, one does look rather silly. And there is also an awful joke that you have to read out. No, people do not laugh; more often they groan. Yes, children are often frightened of the explosion, and yes, I suppose it is a bit dangerous, although most burns are fairly superficial. No, I don't think it commemorates anything in particular, and I suppose none of us knows why we do it. It's just, well, a jolly sort of thing to do and let's face it, it's sort of a festive way of disposing of twenty euros, isn't it."

At the end of it all, and after I had promised never ever to bring any Christmas crackers into their houses, I noticed their Christmas tree, which was quite prettily decorated but which had as its crowning glory, tied securely to its topmost branch, not an angel or a fairy, nor even a star, but – a small plastic pig! I mean, what's that all about? Where does a pig fit in to Christmas? A donkey, yes, or a turkey, even a partridge or a goose-a-laying. But a pig?

Which brings me to the point of this story. These events – the cracker business and the pig thing – made me realise that often we do things for the sake of tradition without ever knowing why we do them. Why do we kiss other people under a sprig of mistletoe? Why do we eat turkey on Christmas Day?

I can't pretend to know the answers to these questions, but there is

one Christmas tradition whose origins I do know, and that is what I want to share with you. It can count as my humble contribution to the collective expat wisdom. I shall tell you why we always have a fairy on top of the Christmas tree, and then you in turn can tell all your friends.

Well, it goes back thousands of years. Santa was in his workshop at the North Pole getting ready for Christmas. There were only eight days to go to Christmas Eve, and he and his elves and fairies were frantically busy. There were still eleven million Action Men and sackloads of Barbie Dolls to wrap. He'd lost the string, spilled the glitter, and couldn't find the end of his enormous roll of Sellotape. He'd had to reprimand two of the elves for abusing a Luke Skywalker figurine, and Rudolph was starting a cold. The elves were muttering about industrial action in pursuit of a pay demand and French air traffic controllers were threatening to block access to French chimneys. What's more, the weather forecast had just come in for Christmas Eve: thick fog all over the world. Santa was at the end of his tether.

Just then, Tinkerbell, the queen of Santa's fairies, put her head around the door. She had a Christmas tree in her hand. "Where do you want me to put this Christmas tree, Santa?" she asked.

And ever since then...

No andouillettes please, we're British

WE'RE A SQUEAMISH LOT, WE British, when it comes to eating. We tend to shy away from adventurous foods like oysters, pigs' snouts, bulls' whatsits, tripe, greyhounds and such like, and settle instead for foods that look safe, like beans, chips, crisps, apples and jam sandwiches (remember, I'm from the North).

Not so the French. There are often items on display on the fish counter of French supermarkets which look suspiciously like a Sumo wrestler's innards, and although in restaurants we always mean to try snails, pigs' cheeks, frogs' legs, lambs' testicles and *andouillettes* (sausages made with the animal's intestines, preferably the colon), we invariably end up ordering a *croque monsieur* or a cheese omelette, and sit there feeling safe and sad and pale and British.

Well our neighbour, Monsieur Barreau, is a delightful old chap. He boasts that he is a young eighty-one, and he certainly has all the sparkle and wit of a much younger man. He still chops down trees and chainsaws them into logs, tends his vegetable garden, fixes tiles on his roof, gathers mountains of mushrooms, paints his shutters, mows his lawns, makes his own chutney and his own *eau de vie*, hunts rabbits, drives on the pavement, and so on and so forth. He also keeps animals. Here in Haute Vienne that isn't unusual: many elderly French people keep ducks, dogs, hens, geese, goats, and such like. But Monsieur Barreau keeps some more unusual animals. He has about twenty of them in a cage concocted of wire netting and sheets of asbestos, and they resemble large, black guinea pigs.

I asked him the other night, as we shared yet another glass of his fearsome home brew, what he kept them for. "*Beh*," he retorted ('Beh' isn't a real word; it's a sort of cross between a 'Well now' and a belch). "*Beh*, my friend, they are for the tarbl."

His dark eyes twinkled in his happy, crinkly, thousand year old weather-beaten face. Intrigued, I pressed him on the subject. "You mean, you eat them?"

"*Bien sûr,*" he replied. "Weet a soss off pepper, they are *délicieux*. One coll them *cochons d'Inde*." (That's Indian pigs).

I had been right. They were indeed a sort of guinea pig. I had another sip of his *eau de vie*. "And what do they taste like? Like rabbit? Or chicken?"

He thought for a moment, took off his beret, scratched his bald head, squashed a passing insect under his thumb, replaced his beret, adjusted it, and addressed me solemnly. "No, they not test layk shicken. They are more test layk, layk..." He agonized for a while, searching for a description that I might understand, and then at last said triumphantly "...layk squerrel!"

"Ah, I see," I nodded knowingly.

On another occasion he came across me fishing the local *étang* (lake) and enquired as to what I had caught. I showed him my keep-net, in which there were four or five small carp. "Ah, *les carpes!*" he exclaimed. "You weel eat them?"

"Er, non, we *Anglaises* don't really care for carp. We prefer cod or scampi or fish fingers."

I could see he was struggling with the notion of fish having fingers, but he chose to ignore it and went on to explain in great detail how best to cook carp. Apparently, you fashion a board out of a piece of acacia. Not chestnut, or oak, or anything else: only acacia will do. The board should be about twice the size of the fish. You then tie the whole fish to the board using fuse wire (I declined to ask why it had to be fuse wire, or what voltage wire to employ) and then you rub it all over with garlic and butter and leave it in the oven for an hour or so.

"And then," he said, his face alight with enthusiasm, "eet ees ready."

"And how do you serve it?" I asked, carried along by his enthusiasm.

"*Beh oui*," he said, 'Well, you muss first cut the wayr, then you tek the feesh (he gestured appropriately) and then" – his face crumpled into tearful merriment – "you trow away the feesh and eat the wud!"

And with that he took a mighty swig of his *eau de vie*, and fell into helpless, rolling laughter.

The joys of French bureaucracy

AS PART OF MY OWN PERSONAL Health and Safety drive, I shall henceforth avoid arguing with French bureaucrats, for the simple reason that if I continue to do this it will surely cause me a heart attack, and my wife would never cope with the bureaucracy that would attach to my demise in France.

Oh I know we have jobsworths in the UK, but frankly they're not in the same league as their Gallic counterparts. French bureaucrats, you see, are specially trained to be unhelpful and difficult. They have all undertaken a Diploma in ABC (Advanced Bureaucratic Confusion) at the Sorbonne and have thus studied in great depth such subjects as Not Answering Letters, Requesting Pointless Information, and Being Totally Obstructive. The most senior of them can recite, without notes, a list of thirty-six documents that you must produce in support of any application you might make, while at the same time absent-mindedly shredding your carefully completed application form.

To them, procedure is everything; the outcome is irrelevant. And because, as civil servants, they cannot ever be sacked, their ruthless and impersonal efficiency isn't modified by any silly notions of customer service. Civil they may be, but servants – never!

By way of illustration, let me describe my most recent run-in with the French establishment. You need to know that, with the aim of having my English car registered in France, I have driven for fifty-five minutes to get to Périgueux, and then spent another twenty minutes driving around to find a parking spot close to the Préfecture (the Centre for Administration). I have paid for two hours of parking and then entered the building, clutching all the documentation that they could conceivably want.

The scene which greets me inside is reminiscent of Heathrow Airport on a bad day. Lots and lots of people hanging about disconsolately, in chairs, on benches, on steps, swearing at the vending machine, reading obscure out-of-date magazines, looking at their mobile phones, texting, pretending to text, nodding off, stretching, yawning, fidgeting, or – in one case – eating a pizza. Arranged around three sides of the room are no fewer than six service counters, at five of which people sit talking to the officials behind them. Unable to believe my luck, I approach the sixth counter, manned – I choose the word carefully – by a very stern and formidable looking lady. The conversation goes as follows:

– *Good morning, Madame. I would like to register my English car in France please.*

– I em not ze counter for zat, Monsieur. I em ze counter for Driving Licence. The counter for register véhicules is counter nummer seex, over zair.

I wait for ages until the people currently at Counter Seex have been dealt with, and make my approach.

– Good morning, Monsieur. I'd like to register my English car in France, please.

– Where eez yur teeket, please?

– Ticket?

– Yes, yur teeket. When you comm in, you must tek a teeket wiz a nummer frum ze machine, and when your nummer is said out on ze tinnoy, you must get in ze cur.

– The cur?

– Yes, ze cur. Ze cur eez the long line off pipple who are wetting their turn.

– Ah, you mean the queue.

– Yes, zat eez what I said. Ze cur.

An hour and ten minutes later, and number 0286, as I have become, is at last called to go to Counter Seex.

– *Good morning. I want to register my car in France, please!*

– Do you mean you want to *immatriculate* your *véhicule*?

– *Er, yes.*

– Woss yur *véhicule* bott outside off France?

– *Yes; it was bought in England.*

– And where woss eet first registered?

– *England.*

– And where woss eet last registered?

– *England.*

– Are you Eenglish?

– *Yes.*

– I am sorry, I donnt spik Eenglish.

– *But you've been speaking English all this time.*

– Yes, but I donnt spik it. Where eez your car now?

– *Outside.*

– Eez eet in France?

– *Yes of course it's in France. It's outside. You can see it through the window. It's the little blue one with the... the... oh God, with the bloody parking ticket on it.*

– Zen you must *immatriculate* eet in France.

– *YES I KNOW I MUST IMMATRICULATE IT IN FRANCE. THAT'S WHY I'VE DRIVEN SIXTY KILOMETRES AND WAITED IN THE BLOODY CUR TO GIVE YOU MY APPLICATION FORM.*

– Please do not get annoyed, Monsieur. You are Eenglish, so you must 'ave ze steefleeps.

– *The what?*

– Ze steefleeps. All ze Eenglish pipple 'ave ze steefleeps. So zey not becomm emmotions.

– *Oh I see what you mean. Well it's not the stiff lips; it's a stiff upper lip, and we're supposed to keep it, not have it.*

– Steefupperleep?

– *Yes. Stiff upper lip. Stiff top lip, if you like.*

– Well you must keep your top leep steef for me, pliss, and not do ze emmotions. And now can you identify yourself pliss?

– *Yes; here's my passport.*

– Eez thees a picture off you?

– *Yes, that's the way we do it in the UK. We have our own photos on our passports. Don't ask me why.*

– But on thees picture you are yong.

– *Yes, another of our quaint British foibles, I'm afraid. As the years pass, we get older.*

– I do not see your foibles.

– *Er, no; we don't like to expose them in public.*

– 'Av you brott a reyssant gas beal?

– *Yes, I suspected you might need to know my gas consumption in order to register my car. Here it is.*

– 'Av you brott ze fee?

– *Yes, here is a cheque for the precise amount.*

– 'Ave you brott your burrsetificket?

– *Yes. Thought you'd catch me there, didn't you?*

– Eez eet an up-to-dett burrsetificket?

– *An... up... to... date... birth... certificate?*

– Yes.

– *Well, it's actually dated the fifth of September 1944, because –*

would you believe it – that's the exact day I was born. And in England we tend to get our birth certificates when we are born, rather than when we attain majority or celebrate our golden wedding or...

— Zen I em effredd eet's out off dett.

— *Out of date? OUT OF DATE? For God's sake, how can anyone except a new born baby have an up-to-date birth certificate? A birth certificate can't be up to date. Am I supposed to get a new one every day?*

— Eef eet is not up to dett you must ask someone to valeedate eet by signing an attestasseeon zat eet eez steel valeed.

— *Who can do that?*

— I donn know. Peheps ze mayor off the pless where you were born.

— *But I was born in a little mining village in the North of England. And little mining villages in the North of England don't have mayors.*

— In thet case ee cannot valeedate eet.

— *Okay. So who can validate it?*

— Somebody in aussority.

— *Okay. So if I get my last English doctor to validate it, will that do?*

— Perfectly. But somebody must attest zat 'e woss indeed yur doctur.

— *You mean someone like the mayor? But if there was a mayor to validate the doctor I wouldn't need the doctor, would I? Is one of us barking mad, do you think? Are you rehearsing for a Monty Python sketch? I can feel my upper lip starting to soften. You really are taxing my patience, Monsieur.*

— No, no. I em not ze counter for Taxasseeon. I em ze counter for Immatriculasseeon. Eef you want Taxasseeon you muss get in ze cur for Counter Nummer 2. And now I em effredd eet eez eighteen hours surty and I hev to closs for today. And you cannot comm beck tomorrow because we are all on strayk again. And efter zat I hev to closs for my summeroliday. Pliss comm beck weez ze correct peppers some time in September. And pliss remember zat your car must be immatriculated before ze end off Augoost. And pliss remember to do ze parking in ze proper pless when you comm beck, or you will get anuzzer parking teeket. *Au revoir, Monsieur*; 'ave a good day.

As I got back to my car the *gendarme* who had given me the parking ticket was still standing nearby. He smiled innocently at me, nodded towards the ticket and said cheerily: "I sink eet woss perhepps a long cur, Monsieur? 'Ave a good day."

The lovely Samantha

STRANGE, ISN'T IT? KATH AND I achieve forty years of marriage, celebrate our ruby wedding, seem set to coast into companionable old age, and then Samantha enters my life.

I wasn't looking for anyone, honestly. Kath and I married for better or for worse, and I thought I'd always respect my vows. In fact, if either of us was to go off the rails I would have expected it to be Kath: she is very attractive, considering her great age, and has often admitted to a liking for Michael Palin.

It started when we went back to the UK for Christmas. I did all the driving and Kath did the navigating, and, as ever, we kept getting lost and screaming at each other. It all came to a head when she managed to get us hopelessly lost in Sainsbury's car park, quite unable to find the exit without asking a sniggering security guard. "That's it," I declared, "I'm not putting up with this any longer." And I strode determinedly into Halfords and bought a SatNav.

Now let me tell you, this technology is awesome. It is so slick and fast and accurate, it borders on magic. And from that point on I received perfect directions all the way back to France, and Kath and I

never had a cross word. The SatNav talked to me quietly and patiently. "In four hundred metres enter the roundabout and take the second exit." I mean, how clear is that? Then: "Get into the left hand lane for another seventy metres, and turn left onto the E17 and follow this for 116 kilometres." Oh joy! Oh brave new world! No more instructions like: "Watch out for a red road on the right and then take a sort of squiggly yellow left a bit before it on the right. Or left. And don't look at me like that or I'll stick my nail scissors in your groin and MIND THAT BUS."

No, the car was silent, apart from the occasional melodic voice emerging patiently from the SatNav. The voice was a lady's voice, rather husky, and I found myself automatically putting a face to it. And then a name. And eventually a figure. Well you do, don't you. And d'you know what? Samantha (I called her that after the non-existent hostess on Radio 4's *I'm Sorry I Haven't a Clue*) turned out to be very pretty and extremely well endowed. But I didn't fancy her, you understand. Ha ha, how ridiculous would that have been! I mean, she didn't exist, right? She was just a voice, albeit a gentle, tender, intelligent voice.

Samantha didn't direct me into position so much as invite me. At Bruges she actually coaxed me into taking the bypass, and all the time excusing any mistakes I might have made. Near Paris, I missed a turning through trying to retrieve a Fisherman's Friend from the floor beneath my seat, but Samantha didn't mind. She didn't call me a cloth-eared moron. She didn't say: "Michael Palin can travel all round the world and never get lost and look you've even slavered down your new M&S pullover." Instead, she merely whispered "Recalculating" in that unutterably sexy voice of hers, and in no time at all had cajoled me effortlessly back onto our route.

It was after Paris that I realized Kath was getting just a tad jealous. Samantha had taken us around the *peripherique* at rush hour without a pause, and when I commented how marvellous this was the muttered response was: "Well, that's all she's got to do, isn't it? I mean, that's her whole life isn't it, just giving bloody directions. I've got a million other things to think of..."

Chuckling to myself, I decided to stir it up a bit. "Well you must admit she's better at it than you."

"Huh, all I've got to help me is this dog-eared map, while she's up there in a satellite with binoculars!"

"Do you have a picture of her in your mind?" I asked evilly.

"Yes I do as a matter of fact. She's a sort of robot with thin features and facial hair. And she's older than me. Why, how do you see her?"

"Oh," I mused, deftly programming Samantha to speak up a bit, "I reckon she's about thirty-eight, with blonde hair and big..."

"You pervert," spat my beloved. "That's all you got her for, isn't it. It's nothing more than satellite porn. Well don't ask me for any more directions, or, or... anything! See if Samantha can look after you any better!"

Hmmm.

Recalculating...

They walk among us

MY DAD USED TO SAY: "THERE'S more out than in," by which he meant there were more lunatics in the general community than there were locked away in asylums. When I was young we had a West Highland terrier who thought he was a German shepherd. I say this because he studiously ignored all other members of his breed and spent all his time trying to seduce and mount German shepherds. I don't think he ever quite made it, but it wasn't for want of trying.

The point I am trying to make is, he didn't know he was a Westie, did he? He probably didn't even know he was a dog. And all the loonies didn't know they were loonies; to them, pouring your tea into your ear was a perfectly normal and sane activity. Their only problem was that they were surrounded by all these nutters who kept pouring it into cups and swallowing it!

So although you may believe you are sane, you can't really be sure, can you?

Well I'm fairly sure I am sane, but I must confess to occasional doubts, like when I dart from checkout to checkout in the supermarket in response to the shifting lengths of the different queues. Or when I add to my To Do list things that I've already done, just so I can have the satisfaction of crossing them off and seeing the list diminish.

Now I know you're thinking that these are both perfectly sensible activities – the former a means of saving precious time and keeping myself fit, the latter an entirely legitimate vehicle for self-motivation. But you see I don't notice anyone else doing them, and I just wonder, now and then, if perhaps I'm just ever so slightly the teeniest bit... well, odd. Or even potty.

I got this feeling again today when I took my grandchildren to Nontron swimming baths. The girls, aged seven and ten, are both exceptional swimmers, and members of Everton Swimming Team, no less. Obviously, I take great delight in watching them flash down the pool at Nontron, overtaking other children and adults alike, and demonstrating their prowess at breaststroke, backstroke and crawl.

But – and here's where I may perhaps depart from society's norms just a tad – my pleasure is marred by the realisation that all the other people in the baths think I'm just another besotted grandfather, as I whoop and cheer and high-five them and go red in the face and scream constant encouragement from the poolside. It never occurs to the onlookers that I might be the children's coach and thus entirely responsible for their fantastic ability in the water.

In truth, of course, I'm not their coach, since I can only manage about a width of the pool on a good day. But, don't you see, I want to associate myself with their success, and I would gain enormous vicarious satisfaction from knowing that people – albeit mistakenly – attributed it all to me.

So I stand there, up to my chest in the water, watching them critically just as a coach would, and every now and then make some sort of gesture as though reminding them to breathe properly or kick their legs more quickly.

Unfortunately, I think I sometimes get carried away with these gestures and look as though I'm having an epileptic fit. When that happens, I call the girls over and quietly say something like: "Would you like to go for an ice cream after this?" but at the same time adopting a facial expression that suggests that what I'm actually saying is: "How many times have I to remind you to keep your fingers together so as to achieve the maximum amount of water displacement with your hands, eh?" And all the while glancing furtively at the pretty poolside attendant to see if she's been taken in by my act and looks suitably impressed.

Of course, I don't actually swim myself, for that would give the game away immediately, so I have to explain away this discrepancy by limping when I emerge from the water, to show everyone that I am unfortunately unable to do my customary reverse butterfly with pike due to a muscle strain. I think it works, and it's always touching to hear my grandchildren asking solicitously after me: "Why are you walking funny, Granda?"

I'm sure I'm not alone. I remember in America following a rather large and flashy car with a sign in the back window saying 'You are following the proud parents of a Phi Beta Cappa Student'. Yes, I can empathise with that; that's really just what I'm doing, only I'm being a bit more subtle about it.

Anyway, back to the baths. I think I got a bit carried away when I succumbed to my grandchildren's pleas for me to go down the water chute. You know the sort of thing: an enclosed metal tube that allows you to spiral your way down into the water. As I climbed the

140

dangerous iron spiral staircase to get to the launch pad, it occurred to me that (a) the staircase was surprisingly high and (b) I might die. But the notice at the bottom said the chute was open to swimmers over the age of eight, so I easily qualified and could think of no good reason why a top international swimming coach should be deterred by a simple water chute.

So up I went, clutching the big yellow foam mat that the attendant had insisted I take, and at the top I looked into the tube at the gurgling stream of water which would float me gently down. Except it was more like a raging tsunami. Surely I wasn't going to go that fast?

Somewhat gingerly, I lowered the foam mat into the stream, whereupon it was instantly borne away by the water at an extreme rate of knots, and I was left alone and foamless. There was nothing for it but to sit at the top of the chute, say a quick prayer, and let myself go.

And boy did I go! Let me tell you, the Cresta Run has nothing on Nontron's water chute. Not only are you instantly disorientated by the left and right-hand curves and varying rate of descent, but inside it was dark as well. Worse, after travelling only a few metres I ground to a halt! You see, I'm quite a heavy bloke, and I suppose in cross-section I must be about the same diameter and shape as the tube, so soon after I had launched I sort of blocked the tube, and a huge volume of water rapidly accumulated behind me. The attendant later told me she's been quite worried when, at the bottom, the flow of water emerging from the chute suddenly stopped, and she couldn't work out what had gone wrong.

Anyway, the sheer weight of the trapped water finally un-jammed me and forced me forward again, and I was effectively flushed downstream, turd-like, at a frightening speed. I guess I was probably doing about 80 kph when I finally hit the water at the bottom. And since I was, of course, screaming at the time, a great deal of the said water entered my mouth. At 80 kph.

When the grandchildren and attendant had finally pulled me out and calmed me down, I decided enough was enough and limped my way back to the changing rooms. Even there my embarrassment continued, because while I was mid-way through my drying routine (twelve rubs of the towel for my back, six for each arm, five for my chest, etcetera - you know, the usual sort of thing), I realised I had been counting aloud and a small group of children had gathered behind me to watch and listen, open-mouthed.

Now these were of course French children, and all I can think is that French drying habits must be different from ours, because they were clearly astonished. Who knows, perhaps they dry their bits in a different order from me (the correct order is head, left arm, right arm, back, front, left leg, right leg, and other bits), or perhaps, for all I know, the French don't even bother to count their drying strokes - I wouldn't put it past them. After all, they're an odd lot.

Or - and here I return to my original observation - could it be me that's odd? I mean I don't have hallucinations or talk to the walls, I've never been abducted by aliens, and I only rarely drink my bathwater. But sometimes, just sometimes, perhaps as I'm counting the tiles in someone's bathroom, or moving my watch onto my right wrist (it being a Wednesday), I hear my Dad's voice again: "They walk among us, you know."

But then I tell myself that's ridiculous: after all, I've never, ever, however remotely, fancied a German shepherd.

Try putting some air round it

I KNOW THE BUILDERS ARE STILL around, in the same intuitive way you know that you have mice, or piles: you don't actually see them but they betray their existence by leaving little clues behind... perhaps bits of chewed cheese or small droppings (the mice, that is, not the builders).

I don't know exactly when or why the circular saw suddenly appeared in the downstairs cloakroom, or which of them is responsible for the mysterious delivery of half an above-ground swimming pool. Dammit, I only want an extra bathroom!

What's more, I'm starting to think that, like inflation and Johnny Hallyday, these builders will always be with us. They have gradually smuggled in all the trappings necessary for a long stay: thermos flasks, spare thermos flasks, a long-wave radio, folding stools, a pack of cards, even a small dining table, for God's sake. A bit ominous, all that, when the job was scheduled for completion by the end of May, and it's now mid-October. But never mind, they clearly haven't forgotten me.

One person who certainly hasn't forgotten me is Monsieur Lavergne, who diligently calls in once a week to tell me ruefully that the *fosse septique* (septic tank) is going to have to be located ever further from the house because of the "slop". I think he means slope. I hope he means slope. Apart from these visits, he is a mere dot on the horizon, and my *fosse septique* looks set to be situated somewhere in southern Belgium. And then there is Monsieur Dubreuve. Dubreuve is not his real name. I have used a pseudonym because I am going to kill him and I don't want the police to suspect me. This is the *monsieur* who promised to have my windows made and installed by the middle of May, then by the end of June, then by the third week in July, and so on. Last Thursday, I decided to confront him once and for all, rehearsed a few expletives, and launched into a diatribe. His response was to look hurt and offended and protest his innocence, but I was having none of it. "You made me promises," I snarled through clenched teeth.

"Of course," he retorted. "But I haf mek promeese to all my clions. Why should you be spayshel? 'Ow do you expect me to feet your May windows when I haffen't yet med Madame Chiron's Februerrry door? Ees thet ze Eenglish fair play?"

It gradually dawned on me. He breaks all his promises, but in order to be fair to everyone he breaks them in strict order. The logic is unassailable, unarguable. And to round things off, he broke into his winning Gallic smile and offered a handshake to show he had forgiven me for my petulance. It's actually quite difficult to strangle someone while they are still determinedly clasping your right hand in theirs. I'm sure this is why the French shake hands so much.

Of course I'm still running the show. Oh yes. I asked Damon, the builder, the other day in a very firm tone if he wouldn't mind moving his foot from on top of my toe, and I said a very rude French phrase to Mr Meyer, who curiously answered by saying: "Quarter to three".

And just to remind them that I'm no mean artisan myself, I've

sorted out both items in my toolbox and fixed the birdhouse to the wall. Again. Actually, I was having a spot of bother with the birdhouse, because the rawlplug I was using seemed to be too big for the hole. Damon watched for a minute or so, and then suggested I "put some air round it, then it'll fit." I thanked him curtly for this advice, and said something to the effect that I'd been just about to do that anyway. I then found myself silently contemplating the rawlplug and actually trying to work out how I could put some air round it, until I looked up to find Damon convulsed with laughter.

Nevertheless, I'm keeping Damon on side. He's big and strong and hard-working: a good man to have in your corner, as they say. To tell the truth, I don't just want him in my corner: I'd prefer him to go out into the ring and box for me while I cower in the corner. So I didn't remonstrate with him for taking the *pipi*; I just slopped off.

Follow the wibbly-wobbly road

MY WIFE, DESPITE HER MANY admirable qualities, has never been able to read maps. There ought to be a medical term for her condition: mapexia, perhaps, or mapophobia.

For years before we came to live in France, we travelled from the North of England to holiday in Europe (and no, Northern England is emphatically not part of Europe; just ask Alan Shearer), and during this time Kath gradually blossomed into an international mapophobic, capable of getting us just as lost on the Autoroute du Soleil as on the Newcastle bypass. Not many families, for example, have taken the M3 to Carlisle or stumbled onto the M25 while on the way to Nottingham.

Once, after we had set off from home to holiday in Nice, she guided us inexorably onto the wrong road just south of Scotch Corner, and having successfully negotiated fourteen of our scheduled eleven hundred miles we found ourselves inexplicably arrowing towards Keswick.

Then there was the time we had a police escort out of Calais, just as we were becoming reconciled to spending our entire holiday meandering helplessly round that most fascinating of towns. Similarly, we have at different times explored the back streets of Brussels and Barcelona, Halifax and Hull. (Hull was especially odd. How does anybody end up in Hull? Hull is not on the way to anywhere; you do not go to Hull unless you are going to Hull.)

On another occasion we even drove onto the wrong cross-channel ferry. And I shall not quickly forget the friendly wave we got from a startled Spaniard as we sailed innocently up the wrong side of a Catalonian dual carriageway.

I think I've made my point. But I'm into my stride now, and I'm going to get it all off my chest. I know that anyone can misread a map. But to become a true master of the art it is not enough to simply give incorrect instructions. The whole process must be carried out with flair and creativity – panache!

If you're aiming for complete confusion it's no use sounding hesitant or tentative, for the driver will sense the uncertainty and either stop and ask a passer-by or else give up and go home. No, each direction must have the ring of real authority and conviction.

And if at the same time you can manage to keep your options open, then so much the better. "Turn left after the next one" is the sort of inspired enigmatic instruction which permits the navigator to subsequently blame the driver for turning left after the next junction instead of after the next town/house with one of those funny chimneys/news bulletin. Better still, "Go right round the roundabout but remember it's the wrong way round over here so come off on the right road, to the left" is guaranteed to shift the responsibility to the driver by giving him what appear to be very fulsome and comprehensive instructions which he has almost no chance of interpreting correctly.

One of Kath's all-time winners came in response to my innocent "Where now?" just outside Valencia. A friend, sitting in the back of the car, realised that she was in the presence of greatness and had the foresight to jot down Kath's answer word for word: "Well, if you remember, it's a... we come to a... like a sideways on to a crossroads to it, isn't it?"

Life becomes so much more exciting when you are nudging your car through central Rome and you realise that your navigator is engrossed in an upside-down map of the New Forest. Little wonder that Kath is often surprised by apparent discrepancies in her maps. "Good heavens, we seem to have got here before the map," or "You must have gone wrong; this doesn't look like a yellow road to me."

I should by now know better than to ask questions. "How far is it now to Avignon?" elicited the response: "Well it's about twelve miles in inches, but a lot further in centimetres." On another day I was solemnly informed: "I can't say exactly where we are, we're right on the crack of the map."

I shall never forget Austria, where we struggled with our caravan (would you believe it, a Compass caravan?) to the top of an impossibly steep and high mountain pass. At the summit, trembling and perspiring, I snatched the map from Kath and, sure enough, found that we'd come up a road prohibited to caravans. The map symbol, which looked to me like a caravan with a cross through it, had to Kath looked like "half a man's face laughing". And after Austria, Switzerland, where I requested help to avoid the road which went through lots of tunnels. When we eventually emerged, mole-like and shaking, from the last of the said tunnels Kath's defence was: "Well it doesn't show any tunnels on the map; there's just a red road in bits."

All this is a pity, because one of the wonderful things about living in France is that you can rediscover the sheer joy of driving along quiet, well-surfaced roads, the air-conditioning whistling through your hair, singing along to jolly accordion music or dear old Johnny Hallyday while absent-mindedly fondling your *baguette*, listening to the happy sounds of irate French drivers honking at you from all sides, and waving interestingly at them.

Well, at least that is how it should be. But I've come to realise that the important difference between the sexes is not the one which has been exercising my mind and exhausting my body for the last fifty years. No, the really vital difference, the proof that I am indeed from Mars and my wife from Venus (with perhaps a couple of years spent refining her navigational skills on the planet Zog) was revealed to me while we were heading east – east, mark you – towards our friends' home in Mornac. Except that for the past twenty minutes I'd had the setting sun shining blindingly in my face. So eventually I had the temerity to ask Kath to check the map. I did so delicately.

"It's just that they reckon the sun often sets in the west in this part of France, so I thought maybe you could just sort of have a quick check to see whether..."

Kath bridled at once. She is really good at bridling and stiffening and bristling and things like that. But she had the good grace to reach down for the road atlas and, somewhat grudgingly I thought, open it. "Where are we, then?" she demanded aggressively.

"Um, I thought the idea was that I did the driving and you did the navigating, *chérie*..."

"But how do you expect me to navigate if you won't tell me where we are? Darling."

"Because it's the bloody navigator's bloody job to bloody know where we bloody are. Petal flower."

"Well we wouldn't get lost if you didn't swear so much, sweetie-pie!"

Defeated by such Venusian logic, I resolved not to ask for further help but to simply keep on driving until either the car ran out of petrol or we arrived at Mornac. Or Geneva. Or Hartlepool, or wherever. But it was too late. I had awakened the sleeping Venusian and she was resolved to defend her honour.

Kath cast an expert eye over the road map for a minute or two, thought for a bit, turned it upside down it for a few moments, then back again, and said in her I'm An Infants Teacher And You're A

Somewhat Difficult Pupil voice: "Keep an eye out for a tiny wibbly-wobbly road on the left." No sooner had the words left her mouth, than I spied it: a narrow, rutted, dusty track twisting off into the distance. With a Jeremy Clarksonish snort of triumph and a James Bondish crooked smile I jammed on the brakes, spun the wheel and executed a rather impressive Martian handbrake turn. As the dust settled, I heard a small voice say innocently: "Why did you do that?"

"Because you told me to." I confess my voice was rising a little by now.

"No I didn't."

"Yes you damn well did. You said take a wibbly-wobbly road on the..."

"I said watch out for it. I didn't say take it, you fool. We want the big straight yellow road that goes off about two miles after it."

I find I don't cry anything like as much nowadays when I'm driving. I think I've heard it all, and there is nothing left to surprise, appal, flabbergast, or astound me. I can sometimes achieve a sort of Buddha-like state of utter out-of-body tranquillity even when instructed to "head for that black cloud" or "turn right just before the right turn." I can even remain calm in the face of directions like: "Go straight on at the stop sign," and I only whimpered a tiny bit at: "Well dammit, we need to come off the motorway here whether there's an exit road or not!" I even managed to preserve my composure when advised: "If the next village is a town we've come too far."

I'm not making these up. Oh no. And d'you know, it's never her to blame. It's usually, somehow, me. Or else it's the map-makers – "It's not easy reading a map upside down. I don't know why they make them like this." Or else the weather: "It's too hot to see the map properly." Or even, as I discovered while we were touring the Basque country, the local language: "I couldn't read that signpost. It was in Garlic or something."

But the best, or worst, of all – the thing that almost made me reach for the razor blades – happened last week. I had an appointment at the hospital in Limoges, and Kath was going to accompany me so that she could afterwards look for a new scarf, assuming they didn't keep me in hospital for a series of life-threatening operations. The hospital is notoriously tricky to find, and I was busy programming the SatNav when Kath said: "Why don't you let me drive? I've been once before and I'm sure I can remember the way."

I was about to point out that the SatNav had said the journey would take fifty-five minutes, which would get us there just in time, so we couldn't risk getting lost as we inevitably would if we relied on her navigational prowess. But I caught the tone of steely determination in her voice and, as ever, capitulated.

The journey towards Limoges was uneventful, although I was slightly alarmed to hear her say: "I think I take the next left if there are two donkeys in the next field." Words failed me, but sure enough, right on cue, there were the donkeys. I wanted to say that she'd been lucky, because for all she knew they could have been turned into hamburgers since she last saw them, but I contented myself with muttering something about beginner's luck and pointedly examining my watch and drumming anxiously on the dashboard.

Once in the city, we came to a large roundabout with two exits, one of which was signposted *Toutes Directions* (all directions) and the other *Autres Directions* (other directions). This is the sort of cunning French ploy guaranteed to perplex a foreigner. But Kath didn't even pause as she selected *Toutes Directions*. I looked quizzically at her. "It's all right," she said, "I know it's *Toutes* because the last time I came a driver tooted at me here for going so slowly."

She affected not to notice my heavenward glance, and on we went into the intractable maze that is Limoges, until she spotted her next cue – "a ladies hairdresser with a red wig in the window". Then we turned sharp right – just as she had predicted – at "the shop with the shutters the same colour as Dorothy's bathroom tiles".

But then it all seemed to have gone wrong, for we were actually on the forecourt of a large garage. "Maybe we should put the SatNav on," I squeaked manfully, but Kath replied casually: "No, we go round the back and past the ladies' toilet – it's very clean in there – and then there's a little road that takes us onto a big road, and then the hospital is on the left just past the tree that looks like an Indian's headdress."

Do you know, we got there with time to spare. And the whole journey had taken just forty-eight minutes. Sometimes, life just isn't fair.

If you're ever following a car and see what appears to be a violent interplanetary scuffle going on inside, followed by small pieces of map being jettisoned from the window, hang back. The navigator might be a Venusian.

But then again, she'll probably know where she's going.

Skidmarks

I RAN BACK INTO THE HOUSE. "Drop everything, Kath," I shouted, "I've got a French letter."

She wasn't amused. "Well you'd better open it, then, hadn't you," she said in her married tone. "It might be something important."

So I did. And it was.

The missive was from my insurance company, expressing in typically eloquent and effusive French their sincere thanks for my loyalty and for all the pleasure I had given them with my most valued custom over the years, but pointing out in paragraph two that I had now had a total of six accidents in five years and associated claims totalling a great many euros (no I'm not telling you how many).

Then, in paragraph three, the nitty-gritty. Again it was sensitively and deferentially worded – nothing remotely condemnatory or threatening. On the contrary, they were proposing a wonderful deal reserved for only their most special clients: a rather clever reciprocal agreement whereby I for my part would undertake a Safe Driving Course, and then they for their part would consider continuing to insure me. The letter concluded, as all French letters do, by assuring me of the genuineness of their very best wishes and the integrity of their desire to please me, now and forever more.

In other words, it was an offer I couldn't refuse. What's more, in the next post, my wife received an identical letter (well, she had been directly responsible for one of the accidents and an instrumental factor in another by causing me to take my eyes off the road while shouting at her).

A third letter followed, with details of where and when our Safe Driving education was to be held. We were to present ourselves to the Centaur Driving Centre in Poitiers at 8.30 am on June 6, taking with us this letter and a fee of a hundred euros each.

The appointed day arrived, and I drove with exaggerated care up to the reception area of the Centaur Centre and parked with scrupulous accuracy. To leave Centaur in no doubt as to my driving expertise I'd decided to wear my cravat and my classic men's unlined leather driving gloves with cut-out back and knuckle holes and stud fastener closure on the back.

Conscious that I was being watched by several faces behind the glass entrance doors, I got out of the car, peeled off the gloves, and nonchalantly shut the driver's door at the second attempt. In the foyer, we joined our fellow miscreants – a very disparate group, I must say. There were a couple of what looked like boy racers, laughing and joking just a bit too loudly as they set about showing us how unperturbed they were by the occasion. Then a French chap who looked to be about a hundred and ten, wearing his *bleus de travail* (literally, 'working blues' – the blue overalls favoured by all French workers) and carpet slippers. And in contrast, an English guy in his mid-fifties sporting a blazer with some sort of woven badge on the breast pocket. Then a furtive looking character with thick pebble glasses and a white anorak (yes, it was June), whom we decided was probably a child molester. And three or four others of indeterminate age and origin, all looking somewhat apprehensive and edgy.

Soon after nine o'clock the instructor introduced himself and explained that the morning session would be given over to watching some road safety films and learning about some of the trickier aspects of the French Highway Code, such as stopping distances, speed limits and – his exact words – hitting pedestrians. Then in the afternoon we would be given tuition in car handling skills, using specially adapted Centaur cars. None of this sounded very threatening, and indeed I was looking forward to the bit about hitting pedestrians, so we settled down for the film show.

Within half a minute the whole group was suddenly serious and seriously horrified. These weren't the road safety films we'd watched as school-kids during Police Week. This wasn't Janet and John looking right, left and right again. This was... well, carnage! Real accidents filmed from fixed CCTV cameras depicting the most graphic and gruesome collisions, deaths and injuries. A man hit by a lorry flew eighty feet through the air before landing on his face and then was squashed flat by the same lorry. A little girl... well, it was just too horrible to describe. There was no commentary, no sound at all. Even the boy racers were silent and stupefied.

At the end of it all, the instructor said gently: "I know some of you are here because you want to win back some of the points you have lost for traffic offences, and others are here because their insurance companies insist on it, and some because they want to be able to drive faster in bad conditions. But now you know the real reasons you are

here. It is so that you can maybe have a slightly better chance of not causing accidents like these. Shall we have coffee now?"

For the rest of the morning we all paid the fullest possible attention to everything he had to say about stopping distances, car safety features, road surfaces, and so on. Never was a group more motivated.

And then came the afternoon session. We were all shepherded into the Centaur cars: inoffensive looking Citroen Xsaras, with their radios adapted to receive the voice of the instructor and, ominously, with what the Formula 1 chaps call 'slicks' – tyres completely without tread. We then proceeded to take turns on the skidpan, an area of smooth tarmac about the size of a football field, covered in about two centimetres of water.

In response to different commands, we turned and braked and accelerated and spun and twisted and skidded and lurched and slid and – I confess – screamed in terror. And not content with showing us all just how hopeless and helpless we were at controlling our cars, the Centaur staff had a few secret weapons concealed: fountains which unexpectedly turned on to create a seemingly impenetrable wall of water, and a sort of giant manhole cover concealed beneath the surface film, which at the touch of an instructor's button would revolve, throwing any passing car into a violent skid and its occupant into cardiac arrest.

We were – without exception – pretty dire. To tell you how badly I performed, I was worse than my wife. And she was dreadful. So when we were subsequently accompanied by an instructor in each car, and shown how we should have done it, we were pathetically, gibberingly, crawlingly, attentive and grateful.

And I have to say, we all improved. But only a bit. At the end of it all, I suspect we would have had rather more control over our cars in an emergency, but the real improvement was in our attitude to our driving. We had been taught some skills, but at the same time we had been shown in the clearest possible terms just how unskilled we were. We left somewhat chastened, and I have to say that even now, a year on, I drive with far more care than hitherto. Especially if there's a manhole cover around.

The day ended with the presentation of a certificate to each person, recording the fact that they had spent a day on Centaur instruction, and a parting comment to each of us from the Senior Instructor. To my wife he said: "Well done, but remember that it's how you react in the first half second that determines how well you will handle an emergency." To one of the boy racers he offered the advice that he should beware of overcompensating in a skid. When it came to my turn he said something that I didn't quite catch; something about taking up cycling or some such thing.

But I suppose he was tired by then and not thinking clearly.

Christmas at Scotch Corner

AMONG OUR BRITISH FRIENDS here in Limousin, thoughts and arguments have turned to Christmas. By and large, it seems to be the ladies who want to spend the festive season back in the UK, while the men would rather avoid all the hassle, glitz and expense, and pass a quiet Christmas in France.

My wife and I have approached the subject by having another of our Family Discussions. We like to share decisions, you see, so we have these discussions. I usually end up making the really important decisions, like whether we should invade Syria or whether the Bank Rate should be lowered, while Kath invariably prevails over minor decisions like where we should live and how we should spend our money.

Anyway, this particular discussion was about how we should spend Christmas. It emerged that Kath wanted us to go back to England for Christmas, and I wanted us to stay here in France. Moreover, it transpired that if we were to go back, she wanted us to take the caravan to avoid us having to "foist ourselves onto people", while I would have preferred to stay in a hotel or shamelessly foist myself.

Actually, the mental picture which appears when I try to imagine me foisting myself onto some of Kath's more attractive friends is quite intriguing...

Anyway, as usual we've reached a compromise, and this is it. We're going back to England for Christmas and staying in the caravan. Yes we are. Really. What's more, we're going to stay in the North East of England. Can you imagine it? And Kath has the temerity to say: "All we need is a bit of luck with the weather." A bit of luck?

So the past week has been spent, and the next few weeks will doubtless be spent, packing the caravan. Now let me tell you, Kath is meticulous in her preparations. Nothing that could conceivably contribute to a successful caravaning expedition is overlooked.

As I write this, there's a bit of a panic because she can't find the raspberry vinegar, and we're due to set off in six weeks. It's only a matter of time before she accuses me of drinking it. But we need to take it to England, don't we, so that she can have a crack at one of the recipes in the eight recipe books we are taking. Kath, who has never managed to cook anything from a recipe book at home, has decided that she will suddenly conjure up *cordon bleu* meals at the Scotch Corner campsite in December, using nothing but local ingredients, a tiny stove, eight recipe books and a goodly helping of raspberry vinegar. Mark my words, it will all end in tears.

And one more thing. Would you believe it, she's actually taking the bathroom scales with us, so she can weigh herself each day to make sure she stays thin enough to get into the lurid red dress she's bought for Michael's wedding in May. Yes, I said May. Is this normal, do you think, or should I arrange some counselling for her?

I, on the other hand, will content myself with taking a few

spare shirts, my trusty Swiss Army knife and my four Viagra tablets.

Perhaps I should explain. It's not that I actually need Viagra, you understand. Oh heavens no. Ha ha, whatever next? But a doctor friend of mine got me the tablets, and I think he'd be affronted if I didn't use them. Trouble is, he could only get me four and he says they have to last me eight weeks before I can have any more.

So I have some options: I could take one tablet a fortnight and thus have four memorable nights. I could take half a tablet a week and this way have eight less memorable but nonetheless interesting nights. Or I could do either of these but involve Kath in the proceedings. I could auction them on the caravan site: that should cause a few heart attacks among our fellow caravaners, who otherwise will have to rely on the annual Christmas Best Decorated Caravan Door Competition for their thrills. Or I could take a tablet just before foisting myself on Kath's friends – Di, Hilary, Pat and Liz. Or maybe save two for Hilary.

But back to the packing. I can see my dear wife struggling out of the front door laden with pillow cases and hot water bottles. Kath takes no chances when sleeping in the caravan, and even in June she will go to bed with a nightie and bedsocks, covered by a duvet and two sleeping bags, and with an emergency rug on the floor beside her just in case The Damp Strikes Up. If I do eventually take the Viagra it'll probably have worn off by the time I've found her.

Just a minute, another panic has started. She's lost something else that needs to be packed. What could it be? The Factor 80 sun cream? The Goblin Teasmade? The strimmer? I can't be sure because she's resorted to the devastating logic that she sometimes employs during our conversations. This time, the exchange goes like this:

"Barry, where's the thingy?"

"Depends which thingy you mean, hor hor."

"I mean the kitchen thingy, of course. Why don't you listen?"

"What kitchen thingy?"

"The one I've lost, idiot!"

Ho hum. If you're near Scotch Corner over Christmas, feel free to call in and foist yourself on us. We'll be the van with the undecorated door.

We are sailing

OCCASIONALLY, WE GO BACK TO England to see friends and family and to let Kath boost the share price of Marks and Spencer. The last expedition was pretty uneventful until we boarded the ferry for the return trip, back to Calais.

Now I'm not much of one for sailing; I've been known to get queasy on a pedalo and I even hold my breath in the bath. And I'm all too aware that the English Channel is the busiest sea-lane in the world.

But here we were on the Pride of Dover. We'd had our final full English breakfast, the Captain was promising us a smooth crossing with the wind no more than Force 5 or 6, whatever that meant, and we'd settled down at a table near Muster Station 4.

I always like to be near a Muster Station, because although I haven't ever mustered myself or been mustered, I reckon it's better to be prepared. Apparently, the lifejackets are kept in the Muster Station, and since there were only eight ninety-seater lifeboats on this boat (I'd checked) between over a thousand passengers, I wanted at the very least to be lifejacketed when we started to sink. Which it seemed we might well do, because irrespective of the Captain's assurances, the thing was definitely rolling about alarmingly now that we'd left Dover Harbour and begun headbutting our way across the open sea.

Perhaps Force 6 is gale-force; who knows?

And then things went from bad to worse. We were joined at our table by two very fat and very flustered people, presumably man and wife. Both in their fifties, I thought, and wearing matching shell suits, earrings and florid complexions. The man spoke first.

"Bay Jove, it's a ruffenterday."

I wasn't sure what a ruffenterday was, so I pretended not to have heard and busied myself with trying to open a little plastic sachet of milk that had been specially designed not to open. But he was persistent.

"We's gannen te France," he said. I was tempted to say that he'd made a wise decision because the boat was only going to France, but instead I shrank into my chair and had another go at the milk sachet.

"Surled up in Newcassel, puraall wor worldly possessions in the caravan, an' we's aall set for a new layf. Warraboot yay's two?"

With a final flourish I inadvertently sent a jet of cold milk over the man's wife, but she merely wiped it off her face with her hand and absent-mindedly sucked her fingers.

"Oh, er, we already live there," I replied.

"Really,' said his wife, whereaboots?"

"Oh, in the Limousin," Kath replied, and then added, seeing the puzzled look on their faces: "Near Limoges."

"Is that near Normandy?" the man asked, "cos we could be neighbours if it is."

"No, I'm afraid it's a long way from Normandy," said Kath hurriedly, and I added: "Thousands of miles."

"Worrapity. We's gannen te oppen a fish and chip shop in Normandy. Me marra ses the English owwer there are desperate for a decent chippie, what with aall the foreign muck they hev te eat. An Beryl's gannen to try an orn a bit by deein' massage an' roamertherapy, and mebbe a birrer tattoowen as well, cos she's got reet powerful hands from aall that weldin' she used to dee. Show 'im yer hands, Beryl. And yer tattoos."

Beryl's hands were, without doubt, large and powerful, and the tattoo she revealed by rolling up the leg of her shell suit to just past her knee was indeed remarkable, displaying as it did a large black and white striped shield with the words 'HowwAy the laDDs' scripted underneath in a mixture of small and capital letters.

"She can dee aal the Premiership team's crests, and if we knew 'er a bit berrer she could show yus where she put Sunderland," he wheezed happily.

I gazed at the Muster Station sign and wondered idly how many lifejackets would be required to keep the pair of them afloat.

"Me brother's aalready oot in France, an 'es desayded to be an estate agent. Mind you, 'e doesn't knaa much aboot it, 'cos the only time he's looked roond other people's hoozes is when they've been oot of the country, yeknaawarramean hinney?"

The pair of them chortled knowingly, then they both started, as if at a given signal, to roll cigarettes.

"So de yays two speak the lingo?" coughed the wife.

"Er, yes, I suppose we get by."

"We divven't. But 'is brother sez there's nee need, 'cos there's so many English owwer there that ye divven't need te mix with the Frenchies."

Drowning was starting to look not such a bad idea. But thankfully the proceedings were brought to an abrupt end with the tannoy announcement that the Duty Free Shop was now open. They both stood and headed (in opposite directions) for the shop, all the while wishing us aallthe best and explaining that they needed to stock up on as much duty free beer as they could fit into their caravan.

I reckoned the wind must have been around Force 22 by now, because the boat and my stomach were both pitching and rolling alarmingly. I debated whether to go to the toilet. On the one hand, I would obviously feel much better if I divested myself of my full English breakfast, but on the other hand the trip would take me further away from the Muster Station. I looked around at my fellow passengers, and noted that all of them were putting on a remarkable show of British *sang froid*, and managing to pretend that they weren't at all terrified. Some were playing cards, a couple were feigning sleep, and one guy was actually stuffing his face with a pizza. It was the pizza that did for me, and I suddenly had no option but to desert the lifejackets and head for the toilets.

They say that feeling seasick is so bad that you worry in case you're going to die. Well let me tell you, when you actually are seasick it's so bad that you worry in case you're not going to die. And then when you've done, you flush the toilet and the noise is as if you've just pulled the plug out of the bottom of the boat: a mighty rushing roar that announces to the whole of Passenger Deck 8 that you've finished.

Well, we eventually made it somehow, and driving back into France (and keeping a long way away from any caravans we saw) I resolved in future to go by tunnel. Less chance then of getting trapped in a conversation. And the weather's better, of course.

But even then I'd look out for the Muster Station.

Call me irresponsible too

MY WIFE, AN EX-INFANTS TEACHER, has recently bestowed a great honour upon me. In the same way that she would make her best pupils Responsible for Taking the Register to the Office or Responsible for Tidying the Wendy House or Responsible for Feeding the Gerbil, she has made me... Responsible for the Shopping. Yes, all by myself. I now have sole responsibility for this all-important aspect of our lives.

In the past she has allowed me to become Responsible for All Decorating, for Car Care and Maintenance, for Wiping My Shoes Before Entering the House, for Getting Rid of Jehovah's Witnesses, and such stuff. But this new function elevated me to a new league of authority.

I think she was disappointed that I didn't shout "Yeah!" and punch the air with delight, and in truth I was quite flattered, grateful even. Only I was too proud to show it.

Actually, I don't quite have sole responsibility – as yet – because that would be too much to ask. I do have to report to her for an evaluation of my performance, and I do have to take into account whatever she tells me to do or not do when entrusted with my new task.

But never mind, I still have a large degree of autonomy, and I have to accept that at my age I'm probably not going to get an MBE or a Victoria Cross, so Shopping Czar, as I now like to call myself, is probably as good as it's going to get.

And as someone new to the art of shopping, let me tell you: it's not as easy as it looks. First of all, before you go you have to stand for half an hour while the shopping list your wife has composed is read out to you as if you were an incompetent four year old, and on occasions clarified with simple explanations and even, sometimes, drawings.

So she'll look up from writing 'a jar of honey' to say: "I don't mean the runny sort that you have to squeeze out of the jar and always clogs up and goes hard so you end up wasting half of it. Get the sort that looks like a paste, that you can spread with a knife, and try to get it with *gelée royale* in it although I think they only do that in the runny kind and get a decent sized jar and if Carrefour do their own get that because it'll be cheaper and we need to be a bit careful since you never bother to switch lights off."

And with that she solemnly and painstakingly adds to the shopping list a simplified drawing of a jar of honey. But because there's no scale of reference, it could be a little intzy wintzy jar or a Great Big Paddington Bear jar. And 'decent' doesn't really help: I've long suspected that Kath's idea of 'decent' isn't the same as mine, ever since I won first prize at Beryl's fancy dress party. So I press for more precision.

"Exactly how big is this jar?" I ask.

"Oh don't be so pedantic, it's, it's... about 125 thingies." Kath, you see, has trouble with the metric system. On one occasion she came home on a swelteringly hot day to find me quaffing from a litre glass of beer, and remarked: "Good heavens – there must be about a kilowatt there!"

Anyway, she commits herself, and me, to 125 something or other, so she'll have to be satisfied with 125 grammes, or litres, or centimetres, or whatever I manage to unearth.

"Oh, and I've put *mange tout*, so just get a couple of good handfuls. I mean my handfuls, not yours. They should be beside the beans and don't come back with garden peas like you did the last time. *Mange tout* are flat, like this" – and she draws a rectangle – "and if they haven't got them don't get any."

And so it goes on.

"I'm putting two boxes of tissues because you're always sniffing and I'm not washing hankies because they're disgusting and full of germs and I don't care if your mother did wash your father's hankies because I'm not your bloody mother and you were spoilt. So get a nice colour of box that will match the bathroom – grey or peach would be all right – but definitely not white or blue.

"Then just round the corner from the tissues, on your right as you look at the side of the cosmetics aisle, are all the yoghurts and *fromage frais* and things. I want a carton or perhaps two cartons of six or eight assorted fruits but not with apricots because nobody will eat them. Make sure they've got a sell-by date far enough away so that they don't go out of date before we've finished them, and you could get reduced fat ones if you like because I'm trying to lose weight. Don't say anything. And I don't want them getting warm so they should be the last things you buy and put them in the glove compartment on the way back because it's air-conditioned if you've finally got round to fixing it."

Then, perhaps sensing that I'm getting a bit impatient with all these instructions (whatever happened to my responsibility?) she throws me a sweetener: "And if there's anything you see that you fancy, for heaven's sake get it. Use your initiative a bit."

I finally leave, clutching my list, which by now incorporates drawings of the pattern she wants on the kitchen rolls, the shape of the washing up bowl I have to get (which must be white), and – inexplicably – a bull's head. I tried to remember when or why the bull's head had appeared, but it must have been after I dozed off.

"And I'm doing a meal for friends tonight so you'd better get some bread," she calls after me. "And don't forget the dates."

In Carrefour I take out the list, which has somehow got a bit crumpled in my pocket and a bit wet from when I hurled it onto the ground and stamped on it, and set about fulfilling my Responsibilities. And, though I say it myself, I did a pretty good job of it, and it only took me forty-one and a half minutes. A quick cup of coffee in their restaurant and an illicit and highly secret piece of walnut cake as a reward for my efforts, and I was back in the car and heading for home, smugly anticipating the thanks I would get, and the team points I would earn upon my return.

The one worry was the *mange tout*. I'm afraid I had caused a bit of a scene by asking where their *mange tout* was, or were. Can you believe it: the French don't call them *mange tout*; they have never heard of *mange tout*, After much argument, the production of my wife's somewhat unhelpful diagram (the rectangle, remember?) the calling of the manager and my assertion that they didn't even understand their own flaming language, it transpired that what we call *mange tout* the French call *petits pois* (little peas). They showed me them, and they were, I admit, sort of rectangular and flat, but I'd been warned not to get peas and I wasn't going to risk 'little peas', so I hadn't bought any.

But my homecoming was a disappointing anti-climax. First of all, the honey didn't have *gelée royale* in it.

"But you said yourself that only the runny honey had that in, and you didn't want runny honey," I protested.

"Well Malcolm always manages to get solid honey with *gelée royale* in it for Pauline," came the retort.

"But that's in England, in Sainsbury's," I said, "not in the middle of rural France."

"And I said get a decent sized jar, not a flaming thimbleful."

"Well obviously we have different interpretations of what's decent, don't we," I rejoined, triumphantly.

"Yes," she flashed back, "I've seen inside your bedside cupboard. Anyway, I don't see any *mange tout*."

"No," I said, "you don't see them because they didn't have any. And yes, I did ask, and do you know what – the girl didn't understand me."

"You should have said it in French."

"I did say it in French, for God's sake. And she looked at me as though I was swearing at her. I even tried translating it into English – Where are your eat-alls? *Ou sont vos eat-everythings?* I showed her your stupid rectangle, and I even did a mime of me eating everything, until she threatened to call the manager."

Unimpressed, Kath moved on to the next problem. She held up the box of tissues.

"I said a grey or peach box, and you've got bloody green!"

"Yes I got green. And do you know why I got green? Because they didn't have grey or peach, and you said not to get white or blue and you didn't say not to get green, so although I knew green wasn't what you wanted, I didn't think it was one of the ones you didn't want." There was a moment's silence while Kath looked at me 'like patience on a monument smiling at grief' (as Tennyson put it) and while I reflected on how life could have conspired to reduce me to talking gibberish like this. Then battle resumed.

"And before you say anything," I said, "I had a terrible job trying to find a box of yoghurts without any apricot flavours, and the best I could do was a mixture of strawberry and cherry."

"Not much of a mixture," she said. "And did you put them..."

"Yes, I put them in the glove compartment according to Gruppenfuhrer Edict Number 282," I lied, "and yes I had fixed the glove box air-conditioning," I further lied, and to round off my panoply of deception I added: "And I drove home quickly so they wouldn't get warm."

This was better; I was clearly winning the moral high ground of yoghurt-shopping.

So she changed her angle of attack and came at me from the side. "But they're not reduced fat," she said in a tone that other wives would have reserved for a husband who had been sent for a pineapple and brought back a jockstrap.

"You said I could get reduced fat ones if I liked, and I didn't like because I don't like reduced fat ones." Yes, I know, I was gibbering again.

"I may have said it; but obviously I didn't mean it, you idiot."

I could think of no answer. In fact I defy anyone to think of an answer to that.

The next item to emerge from the bag was a box of Cocopops.

"What the hell are these?"

"You said, did you not, that I should use my initiative, and that if there was anything I fancied..."

"But not bloody childish things like Cocopops. I meant grown-up things like anchovies, or duck *paté*. I didn't mean toddler's things, for God's sake. I suppose we'll find some rusks and colouring book in here."

Then before I could think of a suitably disarming reply to this withering burst of crossfire, she lobbed in another hand grenade.

"And where's the Stain Devil for removing blood?"

"It wasn't on the list," I yelled, thinking how inviting blood removal sounded.

"No, I didn't write it down; I drew a picture for you instead. See? I drew a devil."

I grabbed the list, and there it was. The bull's head.

"That's not a devil; that's a bull's head."

She grabbed the list back and examined her artwork. "I'll admit it could look like either," she conceded grudgingly, "but did it never occur to you that I might not have wanted a bull's head? When was the last time we had bull's head and chips, eh?"

Even the bread was wrong. She'd said she was cooking for friends, and hadn't explained that the only people coming were our two elderly neighbours, so I'd played safe and bought enough bread for eight. And I could see that our dear French neighbours probably wouldn't appreciate Uncle Harry's American Sandwich bread to mop up their *boeuf bourguignon.*

Finally, out came the box of dates.

"What the hell are these?" she shrieked.

"You said don't forget the dates. You definitely said it. Don't deny it. You bloody well said it. We both know you did."

"I meant don't forget to check the sell-by dates on things, you clown. Neither of us likes dates. You'll have to take them back. And the washing up bowl can go back too; you've got the wrong shade of white."

I've decided my New Responsibility is going to be for uxoricide. Look it up.

You are what you eat

A FEW OF US CHAPS WERE chatting after our weekly game of *boules*, and the conversation turned to things we hate doing, and from there to The Worst Thing We Have Ever Had to Do.

It transpired that Mike's wife had once bet him he couldn't find everything on the shopping list she gave him. He won the bet, but only after having to stand at the checkout while the female assistant wordlessly rang through six packets of 'Tena with Wings' and two boxes of super-strength sanitary towels.

Then poor Freddie remembered the time he'd returned to hospital for a post-vasectomy check, and remembered just as he was due to be called in that he hadn't brought the sperm sample that he'd so thoughtfully and enthusiastically created the night before. In a panic, he went into a toilet and did what was necessary to fill the little bottle they had given him. He was then mortified to discover, as he was being intimately examined by a female (inevitably) nurse, that there was a little bit of tissue paper stuck to the end of his, er, apparatus.

Stuart countered with the tale of how he'd once taken back to one of the shops on the high street some meat that he'd bought and that was 'off'. They hadn't seemed willing to give him a refund, so with military precision (he's a retired colonel) he'd taken the meat from the packet, calmly placed it on the floor in the middle of the shop, stamped on it, and threatened to do the same, one by one, with all the sales assistants until they gave him his money back. It was only when another customer had a quiet word with him that he realised he'd gone into the grocer's instead of the adjoining butcher's.

When it came to my turn, I began by explaining that there is something worse than filling in a French tax return. Worse than watching Celebrity Big Brother or the England football team. Worse than anything I have ever done before in my life as a matter of fact. And it is... emptying a grease trap.

Now for all you nicely sanitised people who have never heard of a grease trap, let alone emptied one, let me begin with a scholarly and comprehensive scientific explanation of French sanitation. Who knows, this might become the definitive work on French sewage disposal. So here goes.

In the UK, most people's toilets are connected to things called sewers, which are hidden away from view and which spirit away all the detritus one loads into them – poo, wee, toilet paper, dead goldfish, telephone bills, live goldfish and so on – and deposit it safely out of harm's way a hundred metres offshore in places like Blackpool and Scarborough.

But in rural France many toilets are not connected to mains water pipes. Instead, one's 'dirty matter', as Kath has taken to calling it, goes into an underground tank called a *fosse septique*, where it is eaten by microbes or bacteria or something scientific.

Not surprisingly, given their diet, these microbes then die, and their corpses rot and liquefy and are pumped out to feed the soil. Then we humans come along and plant our vegetables in the soil, and then we eat the vegetables. You remember the song *Ilkley Moor Baht 'At*? Well, it's a bit like that; we end up eating ourselves, or each other. Something to ponder on the next time you find a chewy bit in the soup.

Well, these microbe chappies are apparently more fastidious than we humans, because they don't like grease. So all greasy water, from the sink or the bath or wherever, goes into a separate hole in the ground, where the grease sinks to the bottom, leaving the sparkling grease-free water to run away through a pipe. Once in the hole – the grease trap – the grease lurks there for several years, stagnating,

festering and getting ever blacker and smellier, until at last an unsuspecting Englishman buys the house, decides he can't stand the smell, and empties the grease trap of its vile contents.

Now steel yourself. A grease trap holds several hundred litres of the foulest substance known to man, far stickier and greasier and smellier than Chubby Brown's underpants, and much, much worse than even people's 'dirty matter'. This has to be scooped out of the hole with your hand (not recommended) or with your wife's soup ladle (definitely not recommended) or with a trowel, into a bucket, and each bucketful has to be carried in the dead of night to the middle of a large field three miles from the nearest house, and five miles from your own house, and emptied.

And as the grease trap gets emptier, so one has to reach ever further into it to get to the remaining grease, until at the end one is clinging desperately to the side with one hand while scooping blindly with the other, and all the time whining softly.

It's then you discover just how many creatures love grease. Slugs and snails and spiders and centipedes and beetles and grubs and things that probably don't yet have a name but are nasty just the same, all realise that you are damaging their cosy little haunt and take turns to attach themselves to your sticky hands, writhe about a bit, and scare the life out of you. I've no doubt there are probably leeches and water snakes and scorpions in there as well, festering quietly in their primordial swamp.

So then one has to have a shower for about eleven hours to get all the muck and sweat and grease out of every nook and cranny in one's body. A bit like Lady Macbeth, really. And all the time with one's wife shouting helpful instructions like: "Don't use the towels – they're clean.

I'll bring some kitchen roll for drying yourself," and "You should have had a good wash before you got in the shower," and "Why do you always have to be so messy?"

But it's done. I now have the cleanest grease trap in the village. What's more, my sandwiches taste better, and I've stopped biting my nails.

Living dangerously

IN ENGLAND, WE HAD WHAT estate agents like to call a garden of manageable proportions. In other words, it was very small. In fact, our garden was small even by English standards. It was best measured not in acres, or even yards, but in inches. And as the Head Gardener in our house, I tended it lovingly. I pruned both the plants regularly, and mowed the lawn.

But now we live in France, where land is plentiful, so our garden is somewhat larger and certainly less manageable. And in it, just a couple of minutes ago, I have nearly killed myself for the third time. Yes I know you can only kill yourself once, but you can nearly kill yourself as often as you like, can't you?

I was innocently mowing the lawn on my Ferrari-red macho-turbo Mark 2 V6 all-singing all-dancing sit-on lawnmower, and I was, as usual, imagining that I was Lewis Hamilton. Granted, it takes a vivid imagination to visualize oneself as a thirty year old in a Formula 1 Mercedes when one is actually a sixty-eight year old on a lawnmower, but I've always had a vivid imagination ever since I thought I nearly saw Claudia Schiffer in the post office.

So there I was, tearing down the straight, slowing for Rotary Clothes Line Turn and then weaving my way through Garden Bench Corner before overtaking My Neighbour's Chicken on the inside and waving triumphantly at the crowd of passing cows.

I was on about Lap 42, and, as usual, leading the field, when my attention was distracted by a melted Mars bar which had started to overflow from the pocket of my shorts. This is the sort of mishap that one simply cannot ignore. What, I wonder, do fighter pilots do when it happens to them at Mach 3?

Thus distracted, I left the Mercedes to its own devices for but a brief moment, whereupon it whammed straight into a cunningly concealed tree stump and decelerated much faster than I did. I finished up on my back, waiting in vain for the pit crew and ambulances to arrive, while the lawnmower/Mercedes growled menacingly at me from a safe distance. I passed the time reflecting on life's unreasonableness and trying to reach my Swiss Army knife in my back pocket (no, not the same pocket that I keep my Mars bars in: do you take me for a fool?) I'm not sure what I was going to do with the knife, but it's the sort of thing one carries around for emergencies, so when one has an emergency one naturally seeks it out. On this occasion, had I been able to reach it, it would have been ideal for prising my ear-protectors out of my mouth.

Be that as it may, the lawnmower and I have simply failed to achieve a working relationship. Twice before, it has tried to kill me – once by throwing me out of the cockpit just as I was executing a particularly daring handbrake turn in the Monaco tunnel, and once when it decided that a one-in-three slope was too much for it and lay down on its back with me underneath.

I mean, I'm not stupid and I can sometimes do crosswords and nearly play the guitar, and I can even touch the end of my nose with my tongue. But I cannot for the life of me get to grips with Formula 1 Mowing and all the other dangerous things you have to do in rural France. To survive here, you have to be able, from the age of six, to fell trees with a chainsaw, chop wood with an axe, operate a strimmer without cutting your toes off, recognise poisonous snakes and mushrooms, cope with visitors from England, eat sweetbreads, cross the road occasionally, and a thousand other life-threatening activities. How do the French manage all this and still somehow live to be a hundred and forty? And most of them don't even have Swiss Army knives!

I've concluded that it's because they actually like to live dangerously. Why else would they drive as they do, or do *pipis* on the hard shoulder of the motorway, or hunt wild boar, or drink *eau de vie*?

Well I haven't come to France to be death-defying in any shape or form. The wild boar are safe from me. I have no intention of wielding an axe or an electric *machete*, or even crossing a road if I can avoid it. My way is the way of peace. I shall continue to keep out of the sun, drink bottled water, avoid all strenuous activity, and – as of now – let the grass grow unmolested beneath my feet.

Except it's not unmolested. It had, I noticed, been attacked – violated even – by what must have been either giant earthworms or more probably, judging from the size of the mounds of earth which had appeared overnight, moles.

Now French moles (*taupes*) are not like their inoffensive, bumbling, good-natured, myopic British counterparts. Oh no; French moles are sly and presumptuous and invasive. French moles have attitude. They are the worst sort of colonists: not content with merely occupying your precious lawn, they want to turn it into a spoil heap, or better still a whole conglomeration of spoil heaps.

So as Head Gardener, the onus was on me to deal with this terrorist threat.

I started by going to the local hardware store, where I was shown a range of products designed to deter, scare, harass, intimidate and – ultimately – murder these insurgent creatures: mole pellets, mole poison, mole gas, mole traps...

Now I like to think of myself as a man of peace, a sort of sleeping giant. Yes, that's me: slow to anger but dangerous when roused, a coiled spring, a smouldering fuse. A bit like James Bond. (I sometimes even practise, in the mirror, the appropriate facial expression for this attribute, though I haven't yet perfected it, which is perhaps why people give me a wide berth in the supermarket).

Er, where was I? Ah yes, in the hardware store. Well, now that you know the sort of guy I am, you can see that I wasn't going to beat about the bush or feign compassion for my adversary. No indeed; I would go for 'shock and awe', the zero tolerance response, so I bought a set of five *détaupateurs* (de-molers). You don't see these in B&Q, any more than you see tins of CS gas or pepper spray, both cheerily on sale in hardware shops here, so the best way for me to describe them is to quote directly from the back of the box:

> THE DÉTAUPEUR® is a trap moles pyrotechnic who operates a characteristic behavior of the mole: it recorks always left a hole open. The effectiveness of DÉTAUPEUR® is based on the blast of a firecracker placed in the gallery. Coming recap his gallery, the mole pushes a plug earth making up the sensor and triggers the electrical contact causing the explosion inside the gallery and kills. Through its exclusive system of vertical-trigger THE DETAUPER® 'works every time'.

In case you haven't quite figured it out, what we have here is essentially a land-mine. A small land-mine, admittedly, but big enough to take out your average mole.

Back at home, I cautiously followed the instructions and gingerly buried a mole-mine in each of five random molehills. You will note that I did this without assistance, and without what they refer to as a 'full metal jacket' to protect me, although I did wear my gardening gloves and my ear defenders. And a scarf, of course.

I awoke the next morning expecting to find odd bits of mole scattered around the garden, but no such luck. Instead, there was a veritable epidemic of new molehills – dozens of them. The little buggers had called for reinforcements, hadn't they, including their bomb disposal squad. And what's more, I now couldn't identify which were the molehills I'd mined. So I didn't dare touch any of them. "Good lord," I thought, "that's worth a double exclamation mark!!"

I've decided to sue for peace. After all, they are God's creatures, and the myriad mini slag-heaps impart a rather interesting textured effect to the lawn. Of course, Kath doesn't see it that way, but when she complains I just fix her with my smouldering fuse expression, and she backs off nervously.

And I've discovered I can just about weave a route through them with my Mercedes/lawnmower if I take it steady, change down in good time and give it my full concentration.

Driving over land-mines. Now that's living dangerously.

God's little creatures

IT'S A DEPRESSING THOUGHT THAT there are so many things in this world ready to do you harm. Awful diseases are poised all around you, awaiting their chance to infiltrate your meagre defences and establish themselves in your body. Everywhere, it seems, there are muggers and terrorists and gun-toting Americans and French drivers just looking for suitable victims – by which I mean anyone who happens to be in their vicinity. Even the world of nature carries a multitude of threats: wasps will sting you, snakes bite you, lizards run up your trouser leg and inflict unimaginable damage. And remember – just because I'm paranoid doesn't mean they're not out to get me!

It's no use trying to protect yourself against all these threats, especially, I think, in France. For much of the year it's just too hot to wear protective clothing, and anyway you look plain silly wearing gloves and a visor on the beach, and people give you funny looks when you walk into the supermarket brandishing a fly-swat.

French mosquitos have learned how to squeeze their way through mosquito nets; our beautiful barn owl takes a perverse delight in covering the entire contents of our barn in an inch-thick layer of its droppings. We are still – in French eyes – at risk of contracting mad-cow disease if we eat anything of British origin, and no-one, so far as I know, has come up with a viable defence against the sudden and debilitating virus which assails me whenever I drink more than a bottle of wine. In short, we are at the mercy of our environment and its inhabitants.

This was brought home to me last week, when I started to find, each morning, twenty or thirty little mounds of sawdust under the dining table. For a few days I did what any red-blooded man would do, and just kicked them away with my foot until they vanished. But by Thursday my surreptitious footballing skills were becoming noticeable, and Kath became alarmed that this might be the onset of something nasty – St Vitus' dance was mentioned, as was Parkinson's.

So I had to come clean, and the next morning Kath was downstairs at the crack of dawn, counting the sawdust piles that had arrived during the night. When she followed this up with inspecting the underside of the table and finding lots of tiny holes, it didn't take a genius to work out that some of God's creatures – namely woodworms – had got under our radar and launched an unprovoked attack.

Now I'm not a softie, really, but I must confess to having absolutely no feelings of malice towards woodworms. You don't actually see them, they don't make a lot of noise or have body piercings or use the F-word, and they only eat wood. In other words, they're entirely non-threatening. I can cope forever with things that quietly and unobtrusively get on with their lives and eat only my wooden parts. Sweeping up the piles of sawdust each day was but a minute's work, and I needed the exercise anyway, so I was all for establishing a peaceful stand-off with our new pets. *Détente*, the French call it. Not

so my wife, and it was made very clear to me that Something Had To Be Done.

So I was despatched to the local *quincaillerie*, which stocks things for killing or seriously inconveniencing most forms of life – mice, rats, bees, wasps, wild boar, wolves, bears, cockroaches, moles, Americans – and came back with an enormous aerosol of woodworm killer. But it was only when I read the instructions on the tin that I discovered that this had to be sprayed carefully into each individual hole. And our table had by now several hundred thousand holes. In fact, it was an aero-table; it probably weighed no more than half a kilo.

For the next five mornings I was to be found under the dining table, dressed in my Senior Pit Mechanic overalls and properly masked up, squirting a one-centimetre diameter jet of woodworm killer into sixteen million .00001 centimetre diameter holes. The wastage was awesome: I forget how many aerosols I got through. And I never saw a single woodworm.

I think I won, because our piles (of sawdust) have gone, and now, whenever I meet a new lady, I fix her not with my slightly cruel James Bond smile, but with that confident, modest, engaging expression that is peculiar to men who have gone through great adversity to bravely protect their loved ones from harm. Clint Eastwood does it well, and Charles Bronson. And me.

So what next? Shall I have a go at the bats that, unable to find a convenient belfry, have made their home in our cellar? Or our doubly incontinent barn owl? Or the damn deer that finds its way into our garden to devour our rhododendrons? Hmm, yes. I can just see myself as a deer hunter.

They might even make a film about me.

Wet wet wet

— *Hello. I've brought this Thermos flask back because it is faulty.*

— Bonjour Monsieur. Eet eez twelf urros feefty please.

— *Yes, I know the price. I've already bought it. I have my receipt. It is faulty.*

— You heff a receipt thet eez faulty?

— *No, the receipt is fine. It is the flask that is faulty.*

— You 'eff brock eet?

— *No I haven't broken it. It has a fault. It leaks.*

— Leeks?

— *It spills the water.*

— No, it keep ze wotter 'ot.

— *Yes, but it lets the water out.*

— You 'eff to let ze wotter out so you can dreenk eet.

— *Dear God grant me patience. Even though I am English, and from the north of England to boot, I do know that you have to let the water out before you can drink it. But this particular flask lets the water out before I drink it.*

— But you 'eff to let ze wotter out before you dreenk it.

– I know zat. I mean 'that'. But this flask lets the water out when it shouldn't.

– But eet should let ze wotter out, or else you cannot...

– Look at me. Listen to me. I will remain patient. I will not vault over the counter and assault you just yet. I will speak slowly. It lets the water out whenever it is on its side.

– Yes. But eet does not let ze wotter out when it is stended up.

– I am aware of that. But it shouldn't let the water our when it is on its side. The bloody wotter goes all over my clothes. I want to drink the wotter, not bathe in it for God's sake. I want a flask that keeps the wotter in until I turn the stopper to let it out. Do you see? Don't you understand plain English? You have sold me a dud Thermos flask. You are thus in breach of whatever is the French equivalent of the Sale of Goods Act. You are probably in breach of European legislation as well. You are flouting my human rights.

– I sink perheps eet 'as a fault.

– Yes, now you've got it.

– No, you 'ev eet.

– I don't want it. I want my money back.

– Why do you want your monny beck?

– Because I do not like the flask. It is not a good flask.

– Eet ees not good? Eet ees a notty flesk?

– It is a very naughty flask. It is an abysmal flask. It wets all my clothes.

– Zen why did you buy eet?

– Because I didn't know it was a naughty flask which wet people's clothes, because I didn't think to ask if it was faulty. I sort of assumed it would work. Silly of me, I know, but I hadn't realised that you were

in the habit of flogging dodgy Thermos flasks to innocent Brits.

– Zen I weel give you a *bon d'achat* (credit note).

– *I don't want a credit note; I want my money back.*

– Zen I weel send ze flesk back to ze fabricatur and tell zem to repair eet. Eff you comm beck in Jenuary...

– *Look. You can send the flask wherever you like. You can send it to Paris, or Peru, or anywhere you damn well want. I don't care where you send it and I don't care if it gets repaired or not. I don't want the bloody thing. It a very notty flesk and I want my monny back.*

– Zen you weel ev to talk to ze manager.

– *Fine, where do I find him?*

– 'e eez she.

– *Okay. Where do I find her?*

– I weel telephon 'er and she weel comm 'ere and sott eet out.

(Rings and speaks at some length in rapid French).

– Zair eez no answer.

– *Very well. I will wait for her, and I will not allow anyone to pass me in this queue until she has seen me.*

– Zen I weel telephon 'er again...

(Rings again and speaks for even longer in even more rapid French).

– She weel comm and sott eet out.

(Manageress arrives).

– *Bonjour* Monsieur. Wott eez ze metter?

– *Look, I'll say this in French so you can understand it, right? I heef bott zees flesk and eet lets ze wotter out when eet should not let ze wotter out and ze wotter wets my cloze an eet eez a very notty flesk and I wonn my monny beck, eef you donn mind.*

– Eet eez twelf urros feefty please.

195

Macho? Moi?

LAST WEDNESDAY I WAS SITTING innocently on the toilet keeping a watchful eye on a spider with impossibly long legs and a dangerous turn of speed, when Kath tapped on the door and uttered the immortal words: "I'm hoovering downstairs now, so would you mind staying in there until I'm finished?" That was just before she lost the Hoover, but that's another story. And anyway, I couldn't really say much about that, because I had recently lost something much worse.

I lost my handbag.

Now during my time I've lost a great many things – my wallet, my diary, my birth certificate, every key I've ever possessed, my patience, my rag, my way, my track, the will to live. But never my handbag.

I had taken, you see, to carrying this fetching little brown leather men's handbag (a malebag?) wherever I went, to house my sunglasses, car keys, wallet, address book, Swiss Army knife, magnifying glass, Werthers toffees, portable phone, out-of-date raffle tickets, used paper hankies, half-kilo of one centime coins, and assorted bits of fluff.

Actually, I've had the bag for years, but somehow it never seemed quite the right time to produce it while I lived in the UK. I suppose I'd

... ANGLAIS !

have dared to use it in Oxford or Farnham or suchlike, but I lived in Darlington, and in Darlington the only thing that men can safely dangle from their wrist is a cosh, or maybe a pit bull.

Here in France, of course, it's different. Here you don't have to be macho. In fact, women here seem to prefer men who are in touch with their feminine side. So naturally, I try to oblige. I now wear after-shave, always leave the toilet seat down, and pretend to like babies. I tell you, if I were any more in touch with my feminine side I'd have PMT.

So anyway, I lost the bloody handbag, didn't I, and it was found by an elderly French lady, wasn't it, and she handed it in to the local town hall, didn't she, so that I had to go there in front of about a hundred and ten smirking people and meekly ask if I could please have my handbag back. And then I had to cope with my wife's withering comments: "Perhaps if you used a shoulder-bag...," "Stop carrying it as though it was a Kalashnikov," "Have you thought of getting a navy one?" "Have you room in it for my umbrella?" "You don't see Jonny Wilkinson with a handbag."

But I'm determined to persevere. In fact, I might just take up my wife's suggestion and go for the full shoulder-bag option.

I can see myself swaggering down the street in Oradour flaunting my accessory, as it were, and eliciting admiring glances from attractive English ladies: "Gosh, look at him, Debbie, with that superbly crafted real leather man's handbag. It's positively bulging. You can tell he's French. You can tell he doesn't come from Darlo. I bet he's in touch with his feminine side all right. Is that an umbrella handle sticking out of it, or is he just pleased to see us? Shall I ask him to join us for a Perrier?"

Nil carborundum

THE BUILDERS ARE IN. OR AT least some of them are in. Some of them haven't turned up, of course, because they're builders.

Now when I was teaching in England we had a phrase for those colleagues who seemed to have a disproportionate amount of absence: we called them 'Teachers Who Are There Sometimes'. The acronym was rather apt.

Well, I have Tradesmen Who Are There Sometimes, and the acronym is just as descriptive. To be fair, Damon, our English builder, is there all the time and works non-stop. And portly Pierre, the electrician, is very reliable too. As are Hubert, the joiner, and Jean-Marc, the, er, well actually I can't remember what he does, but he's always on time to do it. Henri, the plumber, is less reliable and Marcel, the painter, only looks in now and again.

The difficulty is trying to get them all there at the same time, for if any one of them doesn't arrive the others all wring their hands and gnash their teeth and say that they can't do their work until the absentee has finished his. And trying to orchestrate them into a team is like trying to herd cats.

Jean-Marc will come on Wednesday, he says, but then adds a thoughtful *en principe* (in principle). And *en principe* means of course that, while he will certainly be there in principle, the slightest unexpected event – a full moon, a dodgy mussel, a broken piston, a cold sore, a sick goldfish – will prevent him from actually being there in practice.

En principe is a wonderfully useful phrase; it sounds so much better than 'maybe' or 'possibly' or 'if you're lucky', which is what it means really. By the same token, the tradesmen sometimes use another phrase – *a priori* – as a get-out clause.

"Can we run the TV cable under the roof tiles to conceal it?" I ask Pierre.

He studies for a while, scratches some of his chins and says: "*A priori, oui.*" In other words, "I can't see any good reason why it shouldn't work, but experience has taught me that it is highly likely that in trying to do it we shall encounter some totally unexpected problem which will ultimately defeat us." You have to admire their economy with words.

Meanwhile, Marcel will most definitely be in on Friday morning "if it rains" (?) and Hubert will have the windows made by the fourteenth of the month, *normalement* (normally). But which month? And why *normalement*?

Exasperated with all the delays, I decided that if the job was to be done on schedule I would have to be there myself pretty well all the time to co-ordinate things, resolve problems, and lead by example. So on Monday morning I turned up unannounced at the site. Following my wife's advice, I resisted the temptation to wear a hard hat, protective boots and knee-pads for effect, and settled for simply carrying an impressive-looking clipboard and having my Swiss Army knife dangling from my belt. It was ten past eight, and the English tradesmen were, of course, having their pre-start tea-break while their French counterparts scurried around diligently.

I was greeted by Damon, who stared at me disparagingly over his mug of tea and said in a broad Yorkshire accent: "Eee by gum thaa's early. Did thaa wet 't bed?" Damon likes his little jokes, you see, and since he's six-foot-three and built like a brick *toilette* I tend to tolerate them.

Not to be intimidated, I busied myself looking at the plans of the house (hoping I had them the right way up) and eventually they all drifted back to work. Everything then progressed smoothly for a couple of hours until Damon realised that someone had taken his spirit level.

Now I've had experience of this sort of thing. When I was Head (*en principe*) of a school in England a teacher would sometimes 'borrow' a colleague's red biro, or roll of Sellotape, or suchlike. These problems were resolved either by tact and diplomacy ("I say old thing, did you happen to pick up my roll of Sellotape, inadvertently of course? I mean it's quite understandable; they all look the same and I've done it myself lots of times") or else by dint of withering sarcasm ("I'll gladly buy you some Sellotape of your own, Doris, if you can't afford it"), or sometimes by the process of upward delegation ("Mr Cornell, I'm not one to complain but I'm afraid Mr Carden has filched my best roll of Sellotape and is using it illegitimately to wrap up his Christmas presents. May I ask what you intend to do about it, or should I alert my union rep?")

Damon used none of these strategies. "WHICH OF YOU THIEVING BASTARDS HAS NICKED MY SODDING LEVEL?" he bellowed, waving

a spare wheelbarrow around with his left hand for emphasis. Damon has a neat turn of phrase. The level was returned immediately by Pierre, who had been using it to try to reach his bottle of *vin rouge* which had lodged behind a radiator.

I was quite impressed, but somewhat taken aback. Evidently, these tradesmen aren't at all like the sophisticated, cultured, well-mannered (*normalement*) professionals I had had to deal with. For a start, they don't say things behind your back: instead they actually prefer to say it to your face. I mean, how nonplussing is that? What's more, they tend to tell the truth – yes, really! And if that wasn't enough, they usually say what they mean.

Now forgive me, but I can't cope with all that. I hate being told things to my face, and I'm scared of people who might tell me something unpleasant just because it's true. But as the week wore on, I had to contend more and more with the blatant in-your-face honesty of these workmen.

When I was a teacher, pupils lied to me constantly, and I in turn lied to my staff and the local education authority, only I was a better liar than most and was consequently promoted to Head. If I'd stayed and become even more deceitful no doubt they'd have made me an Advisor or an OFSTED inspector.

Anyway, these workmen pulled no punches. They laughed openly when I unpacked my cool-box to reveal the splendid picnic my wife had made up for me, they had near hysterics when I fell into the paint tray, and when I asked them what they thought of the floor I had varnished, they said it was – well, the English equivalent of *merde*. Imagine that!

But the work hiccups along. Monsieur Lavergne reports each day to tell me he is having to site the *fosse septique* ever further from the house to compensate for the slope of the land (the "slop off the lend"), and the unpronounceable plumber keeps telling me what I presume are jokes in *patois*, which he illustrates with the most profane hand gestures and toothless cackles. Marcel the painter has so far given the garden gates and a goodly part of the lawn four coats of gloss and still isn't satisfied. And bit by bit my extension takes shape. Not quite, perhaps, the shape the architect had envisaged, but a solid, reassuring shape all the same. A bit like Damon.

Kath, meanwhile, is kept well away from the battleground. On one occasion she actually suggested to Damon that he might like to take his shoes off and don slippers whenever his work took him inside the house, and if Damon hadn't been rendered completely speechless by this proposition I think Kath might have learnt some new words. So I encourage her to stay with friends or go shopping or fly back to England for a while. I think that's roughly what Damon would have wanted to suggest to her.

Except he might have phrased it a little differently.

I did it my way

WHEN YOU'RE AN EXPAT IN France, British television assumes a new importance. It is a means by which you can keep in touch with all that's going on back home and keep up to date with important issues of the day by watching programmes like *The News* and *Strictly Come Dancing*.

So when our TV stopped working the other day we had a moment's panic, and more so when a friend had a quick look and said that all it needed was for me to fit a new co-axial connection. He said this in the same matter-of-fact tone one might adopt for saying 'You need to fasten your shoelace' or 'It's warm today'. He wasn't to know that, to me, talk of fitting a new co-axial connection was akin to saying I needed to perform a heart-lung-brain transplant, without anaesthetic, in a dark room on an incontinent hundred and eight year old.

But I'm a plucky sort, so today I decided to connect a new co-axial plug thingy. I did so in the sure and certain knowledge that it would end in tears, but I consoled myself with the thought that I wouldn't be short of help and advice. There's the internet, isn't there, and YouTube, and my (unopened) B&Q book optimistically entitled *You Can Do It.*

And my mates are all contactable by phone in the unlikely event that I should need them, although in truth I'm tired of forever having to ask my pals for help with rudimentary DIY jobs, and I think the fatigue may be becoming mutual.

So I donned my overalls (don't snigger) and assembled everything I might conceivably need for the task. The co-axial cable was already there, emerging innocently from the wall behind the curtain and snaking purposefully towards the television. I had already gone to the local hardware shop, Bricomarché, and bought a blister pack containing both a male and a female co-axial connector, and with the help of my DIY book and some withering comments from my wife I had worked out which was male and which was female. Apparently the male connector has a thingy sticking out of it which fits into a little socket in the female connector. This all seemed a trifle vulgar to

TRUST THE FEMALE TO BE DIFFICULT !

me, but I'm not totally stupid and I remembered discovering something along these lines when I was about eighteen.

Armed with this insight, I quickly deduced that it was the male connection that I needed to fit in order that my co-axial lead could connect to the female connector on my television. The relevant parts of my tool-kit were to hand, including some unused long-nosed pliers, assorted screwdrivers, a tenon saw, a prodder thing, nail scissors, a small hammer, a brand new Stanley knife and – just in case – a spirit level and one of those multi-function tools that can turn itself into a wire cutter, a corkscrew, a file or an Audi Quattro. I had also printed a few sheets of instruction off the internet, and after downing a small whisky for added confidence I turned my attention to these pages.

It wasn't encouraging. The first print-out informed me that:

co-axial cable may be viewed as a type of waveguide: power is transmitted through the radial electric field and the circumferential magnetic field in the TEM00 transverse mode. This, of course, is the dominant mode from zero frequency (DC) to an upper limit determined by the electrical dimensions of the cable.

I think I started to cry, but wait – this next bit was better: the ends of co-axial cables usually terminate with connectors (hurrah – plain English at last). Co-axial connectors are designed to maintain a co-axial form across the connection and have the same impedance as the attached cable. Connectors are usually plated with high-conductivity metals such as silver or tarnish-resistant gold. Due to the skin effect the RF signal is only carried by the plating at higher frequencies and does not penetrate to the connector body.

So the obvious question which sprung to mind was – were my Bricomarché co-axial connectors plated with silver or tarnish-resistant gold? I summoned a mental picture of the young body-pierced assistant who had served me in the shop, and decided not to go back and ask her. But it was worrying all the same, especially since I couldn't be entirely sure that the skin effect would ensure that the RF signal wouldn't penetrate my connector body.

Another whisky helped, as did a few viewings of a YouTube video in which a spotty fourteen-year-old American nuclear-scientist-come-brain-surgeon cut off an old co-axial connector and, in about eleven seconds, fitted a new one.

Step 1 apparently was to cut about an inch off the black co-axial cable, making sure not to cut right through it (as if!) but only through the black plastic outer layer, in order to reveal the white plastic inner layer. Sadly, my Stanley knife must have been a bit too sharp, and in my repeated efforts to accomplish Step 1, I managed gradually to reduce the cable length by about eighteen inches. Never mind, it would still just about reach the TV.

I then applied an Elastoplast to my finger and re-played the video, and saw to my horror that Step 2 involved cutting through the white layer just enough to expose the internal copper wire without severing the copper wire itself. Achieving this used up another six inches of cable, but no matter, we could always move the TV a bit.

It was at this point that the spotty American youth reminded me that by now I should have peeled back the very thin metal layer which ought to have been revealed, as part of Step 1, between the black layer and the white layer. But that was a problem, because in my Step 1 enthusiasm I had already cut this thin metal layer off along with the black wire. So it was back to Step 1 again, but this time I managed to complete it without cutting through the sodding thin metal layer, and I only used up another two or three inches of cable. The TV will be fine so long as it is positioned nearer the window and on the very edge of the TV stand.

Step 3 was straightforward for anyone possessed of six hands. All you had to do was hold the cable with Hand 1, place half a metal sleeve down its side with Hand 2, then position the other half of the sleeve with Hand 3, and – holding everything in place with Hand 4 – use Hands 5 and 6 to screw the bits together to complete the job. Sadly, I have only two hands, and even with the help of my wife and my teeth it still took the best part of half an hour to accomplish this.

And even then the job wasn't finished. You see, by now the innermost layer of the co-axial cable (the copper wire that makes up the male sticky-out thingy, remember?) should have been on view. But it was nowhere to be seen, because I hadn't started my first cut far enough up the cable to allow sufficient copper wire to be exposed to protrude past the metal sleeves and serve as an effective male thingy. Oh buggeration! Oh piddly poo! So it was back to Step 1 and on again through the whole bloody process.

But I've done it. And the TV should still be okay because only a small part of the screen will be hidden behind the curtains. And most importantly, I have triumphed. I have come to terms with co-axial connector connecting, and what's more...

I did it my way.

Anyone for pizza?

– *Excuse me, but may I speak to the male pharmacist, please?*

– 'Ee ees weet somebody, but you ken spik to me. I lived for two years een Bessingstuck and I spik fluence Eenglish.

– *Yes, I'm sure you do. But you see it's an embarrassing matter, and I'd rather talk to a man.*

– Do nut worry, Monsieur. I em nut embarrass. I 'ave work 'ere for seven years and I 'av 'ad many men. I know all ze embarrassing sings zat men cum weet. Do you won' some cundums? Men always spik to ze male pharmaceest eef zey won' cundums. We aff many couleurs an' flaveurs. I sink you weel lek ze strawberry.

– *No thank you.*

– Ze black ones are very *populaire* an' zey test off leekorreesh.

– *No, thank you.*

– 'Ow about ze eesy-to-put-un pizza flavour. My boyfren uses zese. Zay are *délicieux.*

– *Look, I don't want any condoms, thank you. And could you please keep your voice down?*

– Maybe you 'ave problemms weet ze pee-pee.

– *No.*

– Lies.

– *I beg your pardon, I'm certainly not telling lies.*

– No, not lies. Lies – ze leetle tings zat leeve in your 'ed.

– *I don't have lice. Please talk quietly.*

– I know: you av ze beeg flettulance.

– *No, I'm happy to report that I am flatulence free. And for the last time, WILL YOU PLEASE TALK QUIETLY?*

– Pliss do nut shout, Monsieur. I sink I know what is your problemm. Peheps you cannot get ze steeffeeness down zair?

– *Well, to tell you the truth... no, that is not the problem. Oh for God's sake, this is all too embarrassing. Everybody in the bloody shop is listening, and some of them have started to snigger in French.*

– Do not worry. I em nut embarrassed. Peheps you would like to show me your problem instead off just tok about eet?

– *No, I wouldn't like that at all.*

– We can go in ze room for you to show me your problemm.

– *NO.*

– I sink I know. Ees eet thet you 'ave ze infecseeon in your buttum?

– *No. My buttum is fine. Well, actually it's not fine. It's a bit sore. And red. All right, you've asked for it. Here's my problem. You gave me some tablets last week and said I must use four a day. But they are big tablets. Look – here's one. It's the size of a large sugar lump: obviously far too big to swallow. So I reckoned they must be suppositories. And I've been trying to, er, well you know, put them in there, I mean down there, I mean up there, four times a day for a bloody week now, but they have sharp corners and it's very painful, and I just sort of wondered if you had anything smaller, or at least smoother.*

– AGNES, ZE MONSIEUR 'AS BEEN PUTTING 'IS PEELS UP EES
BUTTUM.

– UP EES BUTTUM?

– YES, UP EES BUTTUM!

– WHY DOSS 'EE DO ZAT?

– Why do you do zat?

– *Because that's what we do with suppositories. Or at least that's
where we put them in England. Do the French put them somewhere
else? Up their noses, perhaps? Between their toes? I mean, I need to
know, for God's sake – I don't want to make a fool of myself. If you
would feel better if I had a suppository sticking out of my ear just tell
me. But in the meantime, if it's all right with you, I'll just continue
sticking them up my arse. But it would mean an awful lot to me if you*

could just please see if there isn't something a bit more rounded, more location-sensitive, more anus-friendly.

— But zay are nut suppositories, Monsieur. Zey are peels.

— *Peels? You call these peels? How on earth can anybody swallow peels as big as that?*

— You do nut swullow zem, Monsieur. You jus poot zem in your mout' and let zem deesolf. And zen pouf! Zey are gun.

— *And why, may I ask, did you not tell me all this at the time? Why didn't you say: 'These may look to be suppositories, but in actual fact that are tablets that you dissolve in your mouth and then pouf they are gone?'*

— Becoss eet would 'ave embarrassed you, Monsieur.

Don't mention the You-Know-What

I KNOW THAT THIS BOOK IS supposed to be about life in France, but I must ask you to forgive me for bringing Germany, or more accurately, Germans, into it. Let me explain.

Kath and I had managed, with some difficulty, to successfully install our caravan on a lovely campsite on the Côte d'Azur. I say with some difficulty, because the Caravan Club book had warned us that some pitches were 'difficult to access by large outfits'.

Now I'm not one to boast, as you know, but I cannot deny that I do have a large outfit, even though my wife would no doubt disagree. And we'd had a tiring journey. I'd spent six hours negotiating French roads with an outfit with a total length of forty feet and a total weight of three tons, and poor Kath had had to keep turning the pages of her book. So we were both pretty shattered as we negotiated the sharp turns of the campsite. But we'd succeeded, the caravan was nicely in place, we'd had a celebratory bottle of wine, and retired for the night.

We awoke late the next morning to find that during the night we'd somehow been surrounded by Germans, in huge motor-homes. Now don't get me wrong: I don't object to one or two Germans on a campsite – we've always found them a friendly and happy people whose only fault is to have bigger and better vans (and cars) than us.

But as the days passed we did begin to tire of hearing nothing but the German language around us. They would jabber away at each other in harsh, guttural tones, using impossibly long words and putting them in the wrong order.

In German, the verb always goes at the end of the sentence. Got it? The verb always at the end of the sentence goes. So Helmut would say to Hans: "*Guten morgen Hans, wo ist sein ausgebruchtesbannen?*" (where is your ausgethingy?) To which Hans would reply: "*Ach mein Gott, donner und blitzen, ich habe meine ausgebruchtesbannen forgessen, Helmut*" (I have my ausgethingy forgotten), adjusting his wire-rimmed glasses and running his hands through his crew-cut. The two would then have a good laugh, drink a litre or two of beer, and wander off chortling to join some of their compatriots and admire each other's Mercedes.

Meanwhile, their wives, who all seemed to be called Gertie or Frieda, would busy themselves cleaning their already spotless motor-homes and tidying their already immaculate awnings. Then they would wash all their clothes and hang them out to dry, beat their carpets and their chests and hang their duvets out of the windows to air. They might then do a quick oil-change on the motor-home, or at least adjust the tappets, before cooking huge panfuls of bratwurst and sauerkraut ready for their husbands' return.

Between all this, they would always somehow find time to lay out their beach towels round the pool. The pool was actually closed for the winter, but one day, probably in late March, it would open again, and they clearly didn't want anyone else beating them to the best spots.

And they were so serious, and so efficient. Kath was outside our van one morning, checking that the awning guy-lines were still parallel, and counting the gravel, as she does, and she watched a group of the German *herren* clustered round one of their tumble dryers (yes, they bring everything), prodding it and muttering things like "*Mein Gott, der flingenbritzen gebrokken ist.*"

I sauntered up and peered over their shoulders and said knowingly: "*Vorsprung durch technik*, I do believe," but they weren't at all amused. Instead they talked at me in rapid pigeon English. One of them asked me if I a tumble dryer had, and if so whether I had the instruction sheet for it brought, and if so would I them it lend? Honestly, have you anything so daft heard?

The other trouble with German is that because it's such a harsh and guttural language, everything sounds so angry and threatening. Even if they are saying "I love you" (and they weren't) they have to say "*Ich*" (which involves spitting and making a sound like clearing some phlegm from the back of your throat), then "*liebe*", and then "*dich*" – pronounced 'dick'. No doubt they think this is very romantic, but I would find it a bit off-putting if a German lady was to tell me she loved dick. And more so if it was a German man saying it.

In the same vein, even if they are saying something inoffensive like "The sun today shining is, and all well with the world is," by the time they mess it around and get their staccato consonants going it comes out sounding like an ultimatum to get off the campsite before they *blitzkrieg* you and eat your feet.

We were starting to think of building a tunnel, when as it happened Barbara, a friend from England happened to turn up at the site, and Kath decided this would be a good excuse for us to change pitches just to be near her. So we quickly packed everything away, and began to manoeuvre my large outfit (!) to a new pitch beside Barbara.

As always, our tactics were that I would drive the car and Kath would stand outside and warn me if I was about to hit anything. Because I have been known to. And these tactics worked, for a time, with Kath flailing her arms about as if she were a batman directing a jumbo jet, and supporting her gestures with shouted commands such as "Left a bit," "Right hand down" and "Not so fast you moron."

But then she vanished and everything went quiet. It turns out that she had seen Barbara at the washing-up sinks and rushed over to greet her. But of course I wasn't to know that; for all I knew she could have gone to the toilet, or been abducted, or left me for a non-moron. I sat for a couple of minutes, then decided to risk the last few yards without assistance.

But as soon as I moved forward, there was an awful crunching sound, a bit like a bayonet going into a bag of nails. I looked round hopefully to see if anyone had by chance stuck a bayonet into a bag of nails, but saw instead that the side of the van had been pierced by the branch of an orange tree. The six-inch diameter branch vanished into the innards of the poor caravan, which was thereby firmly and immovably pinioned to the tree.

As ever in these situations, everyone came rushing out of their caravans and motor-homes, as if they'd been sitting there since October waiting for this very thing to happen. Kath returned, alarmed, and we began to exchange pleasantries, and inevitably it started to rain.

I took instant command of the situation. I looked inside the caravan, and there, sure enough, was a foot and a half of six-inch diameter orange tree branch emerging from one of the overhead lockers, and a pretty little orange lying innocently on the seat. I knew instantly that the van hadn't looked like this when we bought it, and that something was therefore terribly wrong. So I emerged grimly from the van, and began, without a moment's hesitation, to panic. And keen. And screw my eyes tight shut and clench my fists. And rock backwards and forwards. And say things.

The crowd weren't terribly helpful, it must be said. One chap asked where we'd come from, as if that bloody well mattered. And a lady told me her husband had nearly hit a sapling in the Lake District once, which made me feel much better. But cometh the moment, cometh the man. And on this occasion, the man was – have you guessed it? – a German.

He introduced himself and his wife (because the Germans are always super-polite to show that they are still humble despite being the master race) as Willie and Gertie. Fortunately for him, Willie in German is pronounced Villy. And Villy, as I shall henceforth spell him, then despatched Gertie back to their enormous *wohnwagon* (literally, 'livingwagon') to fetch his saw (yes – saw!) and his axe (yes AXE!) I mean, who on earth carries a bloody axe in his motor-home?

Imagine it: "Gertie, my sveet, haff you remembered ze Axenthingen in ze LiffingVaggon to put?" In case you haven't noticed, all nouns in German have to have a capital letter. How daft is that? No wonder they lost the You Know What. I ask you, how do they keep a straight face when talking to each other, when first of all they have to remember to put their verbs at the very end of their sentences, and then they have to combine words in the most unlikely pairings to produce stupid amalgams such as livingwagon, and as if that wasn't enough they have to be careful to pronounce w as a v, v as f, and j as y. The result

is that from time to time they'll come out with things like "Helga my sveet, haf you my yar of faseline and my lederhosen mit ze monogrammed initials in ze carawan to put remembered?"

Anyway, back to the story. Gertie duly brought a full-size saw and a fearsome looking axe, and together they managed, after about half an hour, to cut off the branch and release my caravan. Which now has air conditioning.

Of course I thanked Villy profusely and even started to say something about how the Germans all had first-class tools, but Kath gave me one of her looks and I rapidly changed the subject. Instead, Villy and I had a glass of Yamesons and to our separate beds went (it grows on you, this verb business). But not before dear Villy had insisted on telling us a "funny yoke to make us better feel". He could hardly tell it for laughing, and beside him Gertie was almost having convulsions.

Apparently "zer voss zis Bawarian who got out off his Bett one Morgen and put his Shoes on ze wrong Foots!" Whereupon Villy his Thighs with Merriment slapped and insisted that we him to his Livingwagon accompany to some sausages and beer enjoy. Villy and his wife were wonderfully solicitous and helpful, and I managed not to mention the You Know What, so we had a lovely evening toasting each others' countries while our caravan gradually with rain filled.

The next morning, not surprisingly, we decided to leave in search of a caravan repairer or car bodyshop, and dear Villy was there to wish us a "*guten Fahrt*".

I was happy to oblige him.